BLUE SPACES

TRIGGER™

The mental health & wellbeing publisher

ABOUT THE AUTHOR

Dr Catherine Kelly has worked as a geography academic and wellbeing practitioner for many years. She has taught in several universities during the course of her career, including the University of Greenwich, University of Brighton, Sussex University and the Galway-Mayo Institute of Technology. She has a second degree in stress management, and professional diplomas in mindfulness training.

Today, she is the director of CoreJourneys and ChillSquad, her wellbeing organisations, and of WildBlue School, Brighton, a coastal education and wellbeing project. Dr Kelly is also a board member of the UNESCO Biosphere (Brighton Hove Lewes Downs partnership), which promotes all aspects of sustainable development, learning and living. She is passionate about the sea, learning, nature and helping both adults and children to enjoy, explore and relax outdoors in all types of bluespace. She lives in Brighton and is the mother of two adventurous young boys.

BLUE SPACES

How and Why Water Can
Make You Feel Better

Dr Catherine Kelly Ph.D

TRIGGER™
The mental health & wellbeing publisher

This edition published in 2023 by Trigger Publishing
An imprint of Shaw Callaghan Ltd

UK Office
The Stanley Building
7 Pancras Square
Kings Cross
London N1C 4AG

US Office
On Point Executive Center, Inc
3030 N Rocky Point Drive W
Suite 150
Tampa, FL 33607
www.triggerhub.org

First published by Welbeck Balance in 2021
Text Copyright © 2021 Catherine Kelly

A CIP catalogue record for this book is available upon request from the
British Library
ISBN: 978-1-83796-324-9
Ebook ISBN: 978-1-83796-325-6

Typeset by Lapiz Digital Services

For my mother, Dympna Kelly,
whose loss led me to the healing power of bluespace.

Important note:
You can adapt any of the exercises in this book to suit
your own comfort level with the water. You don't need to
be a proficient swimmer to do them, but we all have our
own preferences for water depth, conditions and levels of
activity. Always behave safely and know your own limits.
On any given day, our mood, tiredness levels, physical
ability, and even what we have eaten (or not) can affect
how we interact with the water.

    If you are wild swimming, make sure you can get out
easily (and do not swim alone in rivers), assess your own
swimming ability in relation to the water conditions, ensure
there are no obscured hazards underwater and, where
necessary, check water pollution levels. A good resource
for all bluespace safety precautions can be found at www.
wildswimming.co.uk.

CONTENTS

CONTENTS

INTRODUCTION

'Bluespace' is a wonderful term used to describe the watery places in our world. Even saying the word 'bluespace' makes me feel happy and calm! If you have picked up this book, you are likely to be another water-lover and interested in bluespace too. For some of us, this may be the coast, rivers or lakes near where we live; for others, these will be places where we like to go on holiday or visit at weekends. And for some, it may be our evening bath or morning shower that makes us feel human. Whatever your own preferred bluespace is, this book examines why and how water makes us feel good. We will be looking at some of the science around water and wellbeing – not just the physical factors, but the psychological and social aspects also. I talk about my own bluespace encounters and we will hear from lots of ordinary people who tell us about how water has helped improve their wellbeing, both in times of joy and in times of need.

I've worked as a geography academic for years, but over a decade ago turned my interest to becoming a wellbeing practitioner as well. This relationship between nature – especially watery landscapes – and wellbeing fascinates me. What is it about water that helps us come back to ourselves? This book aims to give you insights into bluespaces, how they have helped other people's wellbeing and how they can help yours. There are lots of exercises you can enjoy, even in your own bath or shower at home. There are also shorter 'Try This' suggestions in many of the chapters: little things you can do when you are in or near water, and ways of simply reframing your thoughts in bluespace.

When doing the exercises in this book, I recommend that you read through them first, maybe a couple of times, so you can then do the practice without having to refer to each step – although it is entirely up to you. Some people may find it easier to read and record the steps of an exercise on their phone, and then just play them back. (For anyone listening to an audio version of this book, please ignore this suggestion!) It doesn't matter if you miss a step – like cooking, some people prefer to follow a recipe exactly, while others glance over it and ad-lib a bit! Do what works for you. The intention behind the exercises is to really connect with the water and with yourself, in a way that enhances your wellbeing. These are things you can do again and again, either alone or with others.

Many of the exercises can be adapted to the space you are in and will work well with all kinds of bluespaces, so be creative as you get familiar with them. Each experience may be different for you, depending on who you are with, how you are feeling, or what the weather or water itself is doing. That is the beauty of water: no encounter can ever be the same, because water itself changes constantly. Having said that, there is no need at all to do any of the exercises if this is not your thing; the book is designed to talk you through why bluespace itself matters and is therapeutic on so many different levels.

A gentle word of caution when doing any of the outdoor bluespace exercises: please take good care and know your own limits. Some of you will be experienced and fit wild swimmers, while others may be dabbling in outdoor swimming for the first time, or perhaps in your first winter of wild swimming. The Useful Resources section at the end of this book offers information on where you can go for specific helpful safety advice. There are a plethora of online groups too who advise on social media about using wetsuits, swimming gear and so on. Wherever you are at, just go gently, be aware of yourself and others, and respect the water – in every sense.

Which brings me nicely to the last part of this book: minding ourselves is critical to our own wellbeing, but minding our bluespace – our rivers, lakes, seas and oceans – is something we must do as a whole planet of people. It is our collective responsibility. We will look at some of the ways we can do this in the final chapters.

After reading the whole book, I hope you will revisit it again and again. It is intended to be a water and wellbeing manual of sorts, where you can dip into the exercises as and when you want to. They don't so much form stages leading towards an ultimate goal but rather represent techniques and tools for enhancing our lives through water and bluespace living. Wherever bluespace leads you, I hope you will enjoy the adventure.

1

WATERY ENCOUNTERS

When my 47-year-old mother died suddenly, my world went into freefall. The brain haemorrhage that killed her one July morning came from nowhere, but has become the marker point of 'before and after' in my life. Even as I recall what happened, I find myself wanting to use phrases like 'out of the blue', 'ripple effects' and 'lines in the sand', as if somehow these watery metaphors are the ways of explaining things that resonate most. In short, watery bluespace has saved me and kept me sane since that moment in life when things fell apart.

I've talked with many people over the years who have felt the same way, for a whole range of reasons. Maybe that's what has drawn you to pick up this book? As society has become more broken with stress and mental health issues, researchers are now investigating new ways of looking to nature to help us heal ourselves. The idea of how water calms us is called 'Blue Mind', based on the work of Wallace J. Nichols. Bluespace refers to all kinds of water: oceans, seas, lakes, ponds and rivers. Research is increasingly showing how these spaces can help us to feel better, physically and psychologically. You may already feel this, without necessarily knowing why.

The way that water helped me wasn't instant or immediate. At first, practical matters had to be dealt with. As a 25-year-old, with a newly completed PhD in geography, I was only a year into my first lecturing job at a London university. I loved it: working in the leafy part of London, near the river, but close enough to hop into the city action if I wanted to; lots of great colleagues of a similar age, and plenty of wise owls from whom to get good advice and mentorship. We had a lot of fun, mostly carefree, single and making our way in our new careers.

And then, bang.

I had spoken to her the night before it happened. 'How are you, Ma?' I'd asked. 'Isn't it awful hot? I can't breathe in London, there's no air here.' The summer of 1995 was one of the hottest in years. Usually, my family home in the Irish hills of remote rural Wicklow would be more bearable than any city, but my mother was struggling too.

'I've got a splitting headache the last two days,' she said – unusual as she was not one for complaining, ever.

'Probably the heat,' we both agreed, and moved on to talk about other things.

The next morning, she was dead. Just like that. Forty-seven. Gone.

The flight back from Heathrow to Dublin was one of the hardest journeys I've ever taken. I got the news on a payphone in the departures lounge of the airport. 'Don't bother rushing,' my sister said. 'She's dead.' I will never forget those words.

I missed my first flight and was too upset to speak, for fear of falling apart, to insist they let me through. With nowhere to hide, I locked myself in a cubicle in the women's toilet, hands in my head, spinning with the enormity of this news... Denial, disbelief, but not grief, not yet – that came later. Just shock, I think. I was awakened from it by impatient banging on the cubicle door: 'Are you going to be much longer in there?'

I composed myself, apologised, and went to sit in the small departure area, excruciatingly trying to hold it together. And so, I sat, for two more hours, on a plastic seat, facing strangers, trying to act like nothing had happened. I'm not sure why I did that, even now. The fear of falling utterly apart if I asked for help, maybe, but still having to make the long journey home. I've always had a secret envy of people who can burst into tears and get the immediate support they need. I don't know why I can't; I always thought it was the British who had the stiff upper lip, but maybe the Irish are as bad in their repression?

Ireland: Fixing Things

What followed immediately after was a move from London, first to Dublin – to help piece back the broken parts of our family lives. My mother had set up her own nature-based crafts business on our smallholding in rural Wicklow. It was a labour of love, helped by her early training as an occupational therapist, and her love of nature, instilled in the glens of Antrim where she grew up. The business was all 'her' – her own skills; her character; her wise, funny and smart way of being. Her small stone workshop, her coat on the back of the chair, a cold coffee cup beside her craft tools; the loss was too much to comprehend for a very long time. To try to carry on her business without her was unimaginable, and yet, there we were. My dad and particularly my youngest sister pulled together to try to patch things up as best they could, roping in some local help. But we were imbued with grief and trying to negotiate the new, difficult family dynamic. And so, things stumbled on.

Less than a year after I returned to Dublin, 'the perfect job' appeared – like a gift from my mother or maybe the universe itself. A lectureship in heritage studies, in County Mayo, in the west of Ireland. It was a chance to set up a new programme from scratch – drawing together geography, history, archaeology, poetry, literature, folklore, ecology, earth sciences and more. I've never known a time like it, before or since. The subject matter of my new work was like an homage to my lost mother: it had everything in it that she (and I) loved.

And then, there was the sea.

When I first saw the job advertised, I immediately thought, 'I need to go there – I need to get the wind and the sea into my psyche, if I am ever to get through this.' My dear Aunt Mary uses a northern Irish phrase, 'to get your head shired' – it was that, and more.

I had never been to County Mayo before. It was a large, remote county, the next one up from popular and better-known Galway. It became my soul landscape. The place where I first really connected to the sea or ocean – the west of Ireland's Atlantic. The town of Westport is one of the most beautiful in Ireland. I felt lucky, and divinely directed, to land there. The small town had a harbour with an imposing backdrop – the beautiful peaked granite mountain of Croagh Patrick – and wonderful sandy beaches scattered along its surrounding windy coastal roads. I drank it all in.

Wild, rugged, peaceful, isolated – just nature, the sea, the elements. I could see the seasons change there, and I walked by the sea every single day, usually twice a day. I got a gorgeous scruffy rescue dog called Holly – a cross between an old-fashioned teddy bear and a mini Chewbacca – and she and I just walked and walked. When I moved back to the UK some years later, I gave her to one of my mature students who had children, so that she could stay wild and free in Mayo. I remember sobbing as I drove away from his house, leaving my salty companion behind. (London, sadly, was no place for a sea-dog.)

In Westport, I let the Atlantic air and Ocean heal me. Not consciously; it just did somehow. And the pain of losing my mother eased. The water, the space, the colours, the salt, the wind, the cold sharpness of the sea – it roared, it blew, it shook me, and it calmed me.

A fatherly colleague at work once remarked, 'Catherine, what is a fine young girl like yourself doing *stuck* out there in the back of beyond, on your own? Would you not go live in the town and have a bit of sense?' It didn't ever occur to me to be afraid, or to feel lonely. It was just what I needed at that time. The sea and nature were my company. Plus, I saw lots of people at work all day and had a good social circle – plenty of fabulous nights spent listening to traditional Irish music in Matt Molloy's pub in Westport, chatting to tourists or meeting new friends. But my base level, my grounding spot, was my little house by the woods, a few minutes' walk from the sea. I could breathe and be still; rebalance, replenish and be myself. An introvert who speaks for a living needs her silence to rebalance. I think this is true for many people. When our working worlds force us to be social, nature, and the water especially, allows us to be quiet.

Alone, I could be broken in my grief without any witnesses. And so the water did its job; the Atlantic Ocean changing colour and mood, force and character, almost every day. It became my friend, my company, my solace, my playground to surf and swim in, to walk next to, to gaze upon, to bear my tears or lift my mood.

London: Moving On

Six years later, I began to get restless in the west of Ireland. Much as I loved the landscapes, the sea and my work, I felt that my healing and growth there were done, for now at least. That staying on for longer would be just more of the same, somehow. Not that the same was bad – quite the opposite. But I was in my early thirties and wanted to diversify my career again, meet someone, maybe have children, keep travelling and see what else was out there. Having started my academic career in London, interrupted by a life-changing hiatus, it was time to climb back on board the boat of my 'interrupted life' in the UK and see where that took me. Although I'm not sure that any of us really has an interrupted life, just twists and turns that *are* actually our lives.

I began a new academic job in London. There was a moment soon after I moved, when I was sitting on the lawns of the Old Royal Naval College, watching an outdoor opera performance of Puccini, quaffing champagne and watching a yacht sail up the Thames next to me, when I thought, 'Far from the wellies and the wild Atlantic you are now, Cath!'

And yet, there too was my water: the impressive campus building was right next to the River Thames... and so, it became a place of respite and reflection. A busy day's teaching was soothed by 15 minutes sitting next to her, watching the tidal waters rise and fall. How odd, I often thought, that a freshwater body can be so tidal, this far from the coast. I was intrigued by the colour of the water, muddy browns and greys. I think we are very lucky if our workplaces happen to be near water. Later in this book, I will talk about the specific benefits this can bring us in real wellbeing terms.

Despite leaving my west of Ireland job on 'career break' terms, i.e. with the option to go back, I ended up staying in England right to this day, even though that has not been a conscious decision. As time passed, it seemed harder to return, as if the growth I wanted and needed was not there anymore. The healing and calming had happened and now it was time to carry on – even though this was a huge, often recurring, inner conflict for me. There were days in London where I *missed* the west in my very bones – 'my ocean', the space, the wildness... the Irishness of it all, and a way of being that was easy, connected and very personal. All that London was not.

My academic work took a turn towards an interest in wellbeing – and a like-minded colleague and I began to conduct research on the subject of retreats in particular. Most of these featured water in some way. We wrote up what we did in academic journals and books, and to our own delight became well known in our field.

My own interest in wellness was also personal, and blurred often into the spiritual (small 's') and psychological. I felt, intuitively, that being in nature and by the water in Ireland had healed me hugely, and made me well. I still hadn't managed to put a name to this, but I wanted to learn more. It felt increasingly disingenuous to be an academic 'commentator' on wellbeing – from the safety of a university office and the expert status that is often bestowed upon such activities – without actually 'doing' wellbeing.

I had dabbled in lots of alternative therapies personally – from aromatherapy, yoga, coaching and tarot, to meditation and nature remedies. I found it all interesting, but the academic in me wanted to bring a soundness and veracity to my interests. My university allowed staff to take courses that were on offer within the institution as part of our own professional development, so I chose to do a BSc in stress management, part-time, over the next three years. Ironically, during the course of it, I was on maternity leave with my firstborn son (having met a nice Italian man on a surfing trip!), moved house, and was pregnant with my second son.

Getting first-class honours in that degree while bringing up a toddler, working full-time, suffering three consecutive miscarriages in twelve months and then being pregnant during the final dissertation stage, was one of my biggest personal achievements. My natural sciences degree from Trinity College Dublin and my geography PhD were lovely, interesting things I had done while young and carefree. I imagine that for any of us who achieve things under extreme conditions, there is a sense of accomplishment that stays with us. We can reflect back on it and think, 'Wow, I did that!' mixed with, 'How on earth did I do that?' And so, there it was; I felt somehow that I could now dip my toe into the waters of being a wellbeing practitioner with some sort of proper self-permission and authority.

Sea-Callings Once More

One day, I was in a work meeting in London that was not going well. I felt unheard, underappreciated and taken for granted by the discussion at hand, and in that moment, it was all too much. My dad was undergoing cancer treatment at the time and the situation was not looking good. The gloss of London was beginning to wane, my wellbeing colleague had moved away, I missed home and things were less fun than they had been. In this meeting I hit a wall; I simply gathered my books, stood up and left the room. I *needed* to go – to escape – to the sea.

With that, I got on a train to Brighton, the nearest coastal place I could think of – and stayed there for three days. I found a hotel room, and bought a toothbrush, a swimsuit and some clothes to last me for a few days. Then I sat beside and swam in the sea during that impromptu retreat until I felt rebalanced.

The solitude and silence by the water felt familiar and safe, reminding me of my healing experience in Ireland. I didn't explain to anyone what had happened, or talk to my boss. Nobody asked anyway. I just needed to sort my head out without overt processing. It worked. The water calmed me. I had never been to Brighton before, but it became a place that would change my life hugely. Ah, Brighton.

Our second, beautiful boy was born on the thirteenth floor of Brighton hospital, while I looked at the sea views amidst the agony. I can't say the sea helped with that pain, but it was nice to glimpse it! The sea, of course, is what convinced me to move to Brighton, just as it had drawn me to the west of Ireland. It didn't make logistical sense for either my partner or me, work-wise, but my soul did not want to raise my boys without water. Many people I've spoken to since I've lived here have said the same. The idea of a 'childhood by the sea' is something I've looked at in my academic research too, and it is a common family motivation: to live by, or to create family holiday memories by the sea.

Pushing my baby son along the seafront with the wind in my hair felt right. I had the sea again, and it was good. My now three-year-old first-born boy and I played with the pebbles on the beach for hours, throwing them in the water, piling them up and knocking them down. Life in the years that have followed has been a mixture of commuting, growing, school, friendships and the sea – a constant everyday backdrop to it all. Our holidays are always to places where we can surf or snorkel – in Cornwall, Devon, Portugal, Lanzarote or Greece – and our children have grown to love the water and waves as much as I do.

My academic work in recent years has turned to a quest to understand this relationship between nature and wellbeing. And in particular, this relationship between the sea and wellbeing. While working at a local university temporarily, I was lucky enough to meet the late Martin Jordan, an ecotherapist (i.e. a psychotherapist with a speciality in nature and healing) who was publishing in this newly emerging field.

When I heard him give a talk one evening, he described how, as a child, nature had been his *companion* while things at home were hard; and this resonated strongly with my own Irish childhood. As I read more about nature connections, place attachment and other theories, a light of recognition switched on in my mind. From there, I began to study and research more about this idea of nature and healing, and the relationship between people, place and environment. Suddenly, I had the words, concepts and frameworks to explain what I had intuitively felt for so long. It felt exciting! I'm sure many of you have experienced this too, in your own growing-up? A love of nature and the water gives us companionship for life, I think.

In a coming together of my personal journey (I hate that term, but in this case it was true, literally), my academic profession and my own practice, things began to make sense and converge. I could almost hear a metaphorical clicking sound. In addition to my academic work, I undertook training first in mindfulness and then in mindfulness for young people. I felt really strongly about giving kids the tools to feel strong inside. And so, I launched 'ChillSquad' in Brighton, my own wellbeing, mindfulness and resilience programme for children, teachers and families. It took all my courage to approach schools to see if they wanted to run my programme and to venture out into my own work.

Up until this point, I could hide, in some sense, behind my doctoral title and university affiliation. I hadn't realised how much of a shield that was, or indeed what a conduit it was too for easy introductions to open doors. But here I was, just me, nervously asking to be allowed in, to speak to children at school and to help them with their own wellbeing and resilience. It was soul-baring and I felt very vulnerable.

Luckily, it all paid off, and I have now taught over a thousand young people as part of in-school programmes, clubs and weekend workshops for children, families and parents. I've also run many training workshops to show teachers, social workers or anyone working with young people how to teach my ChillSquad programme. These training retreats are some of the loveliest, most bonding and humbling experiences of my professional career. There is an openness, power and connection during those courses that I can't quite verbalise. I would really advise anyone who wants a new work direction to follow their intuition, soul or desires, even if only in a small way to start with. Giving it a shot is something you will never regret. Doing something you feel you are meant to do scratches a soul-itch like nothing else!

During my early years in Brighton, I also did a course in 'wild beach school' with the lovely Sussex Wildlife Trust. This gave me lots of ideas, and equipped with those and my long experience in teaching geography and earth sciences, I started my own WildBlue School in Brighton. Today, both the WildBlue School and ChillSquad fit in alongside my part-time academic job. All of this allows me to combine my research and practice in water and wellbeing.

WildBlue School is a wonderfully fulfilling outdoor joy! I take 30 to 100 children to the beach on field-days in the summer term, and also run holiday camps and occasional events where we learn about the coast as both a natural and a human environment, along with identification skills, crafts and mindfulness exercises. I've also started a 'Soul Saturdays by the Sea' micro-break for busy women in Brighton and beyond. The need to retreat, especially by the sea, is something I really want to share with others. We will explore some of these wellbeing practices later in the book.

Watching children's joy and relief as they get outdoors to the sea is as humbling as it is awesome. I'm sure many parents reading this have witnessed it too. A child's total mindfulness in present-moment enthusiasm could teach us all a lot. I love my university students dearly, but seeing younger children respond instantly and wholeheartedly by the sea, or in a ChillSquad session, gives me a sense of work fulfilment I had never dared to hope for. As the west of Ireland felt like my soul landscape, this feels like my soul work.

Bringing It All Together

Which brings me to the final piece of the current jigsaw puzzle: wild swimming. As I didn't grow up right next to the sea, this is not something I have always done, but people always ask me if I have. People connect to bluespace at different times in their lives; not everyone is 'born into it' and it really doesn't matter when or how you come to love it. The main thing is that you enjoy it. In the chapters to come, I will talk about my early starts in

Irish rivers, learning to surf in Cornwall and a near-death experience in African white water.

However, one of the greatest joys for me in recent years has been becoming part of a unique wild swimming group called the 'Salty Seabirds' in Brighton. Started by two amazing women, Kath and Cath, as a social enterprise, its ethos is simply 'salted wellbeing'. I'll be talking more about the Salty Seabirds in Chapters 2 and 3, and how they help women from all backgrounds to access the water. My involvement with this group of amazing (mainly) women, who share a passion for bluespace, has been the icing on the cake in terms of my own Brighton adventure.

All of which brings me to a nexus of sorts. My own personal experiences – as an academic, setting up ChillSquad and WildBlue School, training in stress management and mindfulness, publishing academic papers about wellbeing and nature, and becoming a proud Seabird wild swimmer – have all really led me to this point and to writing this book. I often feel a bit of an oddity: not quite one thing or another; not a 'serious, stern-faced academic' nor a full-time practitioner, not a hippy or guru, nor a super-fit and accomplished swimmer… but little bits of everything. That has made me feel like I never quite fit in anywhere, or into any one box, but equally, my general and broad interests have a fluidity that have served me well.

Now that you have heard my story, I hope some of these experiences resonate with your own life. Have you had any kind of grief, physical or psychological pain eased by water in nature? Do you find that it makes you feel better? That it takes away pain? Quietens your mind? Makes you feel more connected? Brings some kind of relief or, indeed, release? What follows in this book is a mix of accessible science and research into wellbeing, bluespace and Blue Mind ideas; an examination of various types of bluespace (including rivers, lakes, seas and oceans) and how they can make us feel well.

There will be a mixture of discussion, evidence, personal stories and practical exercises you can do yourself in these spaces – for breathing, mindfulness and more. We will look at the geography of these watery places, hear from regular people about how these places have helped them too, how they can help you and, finally, how we can all help to look after the bluespaces that matter so much to us.

2

WATER AND WELLBEING:
WHAT WE KNOW SO FAR

If you had said to me 25 years ago that I would be writing a book about the love, science and practice of water and wellbeing, I would probably have raised a cynical eyebrow. My own life has pretty much led me to write this book, but it is also a sign of the times we are living in now. Today, we work, live and play in a time-pressured and frenetic society, where we are now looking for new strategies to help us cope with burgeoning levels of poor mental wellbeing and stress. Our health systems are stretched to capacity and drug prescriptions for antidepressants and anxiety medication are at an all-time high. In this chapter, I'd like to have a conversation with you about what wellbeing means, how stress affects us and, most of all, how natural, watery 'bluespaces' can help us to feel well and/or create a state of calm 'blue mind'. I will talk about *some of* the existing writing and research that has been conducted so far in this area. It's a light-touch approach, hopefully accessible and easy to read, without trying to say all there is to say about every piece of work that has gone before. So let's get started.

What is Wellbeing?

I suppose we could say that wellbeing is central in our relationship with water, even though this may not be an intentional aim of our being in or near bluespace. 'Wellbeing' is a term that has been bandied about a lot in recent times – some loathe the phrase, while others are fine with it. Originally, the term 'wellness' was popular, which is a merging of the words 'wellbeing' and 'wholeness'. So, wellbeing, then, is a state in which our whole selves feel well or balanced. We can talk about physical wellbeing, psychological or mental wellbeing, economic wellbeing and social wellbeing, to name a few types. Ideally, in order to function in an optimal way, all of these different elements would be in a positive state for any one individual. However, I think it's pretty unrealistic for us to exist in a constant state of positive wellbeing across all these areas. Life has its ups and downs – and for many of us, each single day can have lots of ups and downs too!

A whole myriad of wellbeing debates, measures and definitions exist in both academic and emerging policy literature. Put simply, wellbeing refers to the status of an individual or population where body, mind and spirit are in balance, and there is an absence of illness. It implies *proactive strategies* for staying physically, psychologically and/or spiritually 'well'.

Now, there are different ways we can describe and assess wellbeing. 'Subjective wellbeing' (or personal wellbeing) asks people directly how they think and feel about their *own* wellbeing, and includes aspects such as life satisfaction, positive *emotions* ('hedonic wellbeing'), and whether they feel their life is *meaningful* ('eudemonic wellbeing'). Improving our subjective wellbeing is a worthy goal in its own right, but it can be instrumental to other outcomes too, such as better physical health, engaging with our work, and personal creativity or productivity. 'Objective wellbeing', on the other hand, is easier to measure. It is based on assumptions about basic human needs and rights, including aspects such as adequate food, shelter, physical health, education, safety and so on. Objective wellbeing can be measured through self-report (e.g., asking people whether they have a specific health condition), or through more objective measures (e.g., mortality rates, housing quality, income and life expectancy). Objective wellbeing measurements can be compared across large populations, whilst subjective wellbeing measurements are more insightful but less applicable across large numbers of people, due to the specific and personal nature of our individual experiences.

Research from the UK Department of Health shows that wellbeing:

- adds years to life and improves recovery from illness;
- is associated with positive health behaviours in adults and children;
- influences the wellbeing and mental health of those close to us;
- may ultimately reduce the healthcare burden;

and that:

- parents' mental health and wellbeing are strongly associated with their children's.[1]

We can see, therefore, that levels of wellbeing play a major role in how we live our lives, how we navigate our own journeys and maybe even the extent to which we are 'thriving versus surviving'.

So how do we know if our own wellbeing is OK? Short of going for a full (physical) assessment with our doctor, a good tool to check in with ourselves and how well we feel, is to complete a 'wellness wheel' once a month or so. I do this to help me keep track of those areas I need to give some *attention* to in my own life. I don't really advocate the use of the words 'fix' or 'improve' here, as that can feel pressured; it's more of a gentle self-nudging on those areas that we may intuitively know need some care in our lives.

Try This

Have a go at evaluating your own wellbeing right now, using the wheel on the following page. Score yourself a '5' for optimal evaluation (everything in this area of your life is amazing!), or a '1' if it is very poor... Using

the dots on the 'spokes' of the wheel, place an X on
the number that best reflects each factor in your life,
right now. The number 1 sits closest to the centre of
the wheel, while 5 is on the outside rim, and the dots in
between represent the scores 2, 3 and 4.

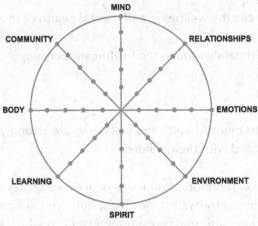

The Wellbeing Wheel[2]

How did you do? What message do you hear when you
look at your own evaluation? Ideally you are aiming for
a balanced and high-scoring wheel. An evenly balanced
wheel turns more easily, right? If there are lots of jags,
or ins and outs, then sit quietly and reflect on what this
says about your own life. Take a breath, and listen.

One of the side-effects of our modern, busy lives is that we
don't often stop to check in with ourselves about our own
wellbeing levels. If you can, I'd really recommend taking
yourself away from home for 24 hours (from Saturday
lunchtime to Sunday lunchtime often has minimal impact
on family life, for example) with a journal (and swimsuit of
course!), and create a small mini-retreat for yourself to do
this exercise. I do it myself every four months – and it is
one of the ways in which I've improved much of my own

wellbeing and life-purpose direction. More of this in 'Solo Retreat by the Water' on page 110.

When we speak about wellbeing, there is often a difference in how we talk to ourselves or our friends about our wellbeing (for example, we may use phrases such as 'I'm exhausted' or 'I hate my job') and how policy-makers, researchers or organisations discuss it. There is now a plethora of advice, strategies and many potential therapies on offer out there. I won't attempt here to assess or critique government wellbeing policies, nor to review every therapeutic intervention – it's just too big and unwieldy a topic! There are those who would say, rightly, that if we lived in a world with less inequality, where everyone had access to well-paid and safe work and proper social support, good housing and education, many wellbeing policies would never be needed in the first place. There is truth in this: the structural base of Western society is all too often broken, uneven and flawed. What I do know, and what I have taught others and experienced first-hand myself, is that nature, water and breathing all help us to cope a little better with our own moment-by-moment realities, whatever they may be.

A commonly used approach by many organisations to frame how wellbeing can be worked towards is the 'Five Ways to Wellbeing' concept devised by the New Economics Foundation (NEF).[3] These are:

1 connect;
2 be active;
3 take notice;
4 keep learning;
5 give.

These five elements can be applied to our relationship with water in many ways; for example:

- *connecting* with others or with oneself by the sea for psycho-social outcomes;

- physical *activity* for water and land-based sports/activities;
- *noticing* our own mood when we need to get to bluespace, and also noticing our surroundings while we are there: the colour and movement of the water, the feel of it;
- *learning* about the coast as a human and natural environment;
- *giving* time and expertise to help look after each other, or indeed, the aquatic environment itself through organised or voluntary efforts.

Connecting these five elements in a human-environment symbiotic way (i.e. 'bluespace looks after me, so I will look after it!') can increase our own levels of wellbeing and the wellbeing of bluespaces themselves.

I've always thought that there are strong commonalities between the areas of environmental/marine policy and wellbeing strategies: a strong ethos of caregiving, of paying attention, of education or growth, of sustainable behaviour (of the self, and in relation to the environment), of legacy and of community action. What we can see in many of us who love water is, indeed, this sense of wanting to look after it – it being our playground and, for many, our source of community and wellbeing. I've conducted various research studies myself into why and how water makes us feel well, the relationships between our love of the sea and our need to look after it, and how mindfulness by the sea improves our wellbeing. I have also conducted a study on the ideas of emotions, quality time and how being by or in the water makes us feel like our 'real selves'. More of this throughout the book, but here is a sample smattering of some of the feelings people have about water:

I love the numbing shock of stepping into frigid, grey, rough seas on a cold morning, and the utter freedom that comes when I relax into the cold and float... The feeling of being safe and protected from anything that worried me just a moment before.

I love being near the sea, in the sea, looking at the sea. During the pandemic lockdown, I missed the screaming, laughing, swearing and outright dithering I did before finally getting in. I missed the fact I felt like I finally found my lost little self in the sea, something I didn't even know I was looking for. In fact, I probably felt the most peaceful I ever have, and I just missed it.

The feel of the water as I step in is important – like a cuddle... I love the smell of fresh open water, the sounds of the water moving and the small, quiet sounds of nature as I gently swim or float by. It has never failed to help soothe me; nothing else gets close to the relief I feel when I first get into the river. When in therapy, I visualised my first thirty seconds of river entry and swimming as my go-to 'happy place'.

So, we can see that the whole area of wellbeing has lots of different elements to it: how we define it, how we measure it and how we react to it at policy, societal and personal levels. What matters most, I often think, is how we ourselves feel. And water can help us to *feel well*. What we can do individually is try to notice when our wellbeing drops, what happens to us, and then to consider which actions we are taking or could take in response.

Before I go on to talk specifically about water and wellbeing, I want to briefly discuss stress, because stress affects how our bodies and minds operate at variable levels of wellbeing. This is important when we are trying to understand the positive effect water has on us, in all the different wellbeing categories we've looked at so far – those of physical, psychological and social wellbeing.

Stress

Stress and anxiety are bedpartners in many ways, and they have a huge effect on both our physical and our psychological wellbeing. Our body and mind are closely related. When we feel anxious or worried, this tends to show up physically in certain aches and ailments. There are many scientific definitions of stress, but very simply, stress happens 'when the pressures on any one person exceed that person's perceived ability to cope with them'.[4] 'Perceived' is the important word here… what you see as being easy, someone else may find very hard to cope with. How often has a partner or a friend looked askance at you while you've struggled with something they would shrug off? Our own ability to cope depends on many things – our genetic make-up, the lives we've led, the coping strategies we have learned (or not), and our ability to ask for help.

Scientifically, anxiety and stress show up in the sympathetic nervous system in our bodies (the SNS): this is our 'flight, fight or freeze' response. When stress is triggered in the amygdalae (the panic-response station) parts of our brains, our breathing becomes faster; our blood pressure rises; we may sweat, or become light-headed; and the body releases high levels of cortisol and adrenaline – which are not good for us (unless there is a real and immediate emergency). For some people some of the time, responses to reduce stress may be positive – we might try to improve our nutrition, eat better, or exercise – but for many, there is a negative response, such as increased snacking, comfort eating or drinking. This creates a vicious circle scenario: our bodies are not only trying to cope with increased levels of stress hormones, they are also then having to deal with the toxins or low-grade food we are feeding them. Not a great scenario!

The good news is that inside our bodies we also have the 'PNS' – the parasympathetic nervous system. This is our 'rest and repair' system. We don't have to do anything to kick-start it, it is just *there*… We do, however, need to give it a chance to work – which it cannot do, effectively, if the SNS 'alarm button' is being hit constantly in our bodies and minds through continued levels of stress. The PNS is optimised when we are in a state of calm, or in deep sleep. Busy lives and juggling anxiety over family, relationships, our income or mental health all mean that as a society many of us are living in regular states of emergency in terms of how our brain translates and responds to the messages we are sending it.

Our PNS calms us down and allows the cells in our body to repair – especially our T-cells, which form an essential part of our immune response. Ironically, being physically and mentally stressed and not sleeping well further reduce our ability to fight illness. So, activating our sympathetic nervous system over and over again actually supresses our immune system, because it competes with our PNS and dilutes its effectiveness. Psychoneuroimmunology is a field of science that examines this relationship between our state of mind (e.g. anxiety/stress), our nervous system and our ability to be well. I won't go into this here but the take-out message is that stressed bodies and minds don't perform well or feel well to be in!

Try This

Earlier, we looked at some of the general ways in which we can improve our wellbeing (e.g. the Five Ways to Wellbeing). But the most immediate, effective and free way that you, individually, can reduce your stress levels is to focus on your breathing. Yes, just take a few big deep breaths. This is not hippy nonsense – it is firmly rooted in neuroscience. Very simply, taking several deep breaths cuts the panic signal to your brain's amygdalae and allows your PNS (parasympathetic nervous system) to take over and do its job. Regulating your breathing, deliberately, is one of the best things you can do for your own wellbeing.

The calming effect of regulating our breathing is why, if we ever feel panicky in water, the best thing we can do is to try to float and breathe, as counter-intuitive as it might seem. Our deep breath allows the PNS and our prefrontal cortex part of the brain (which controls calm, clear thinking) to figure out what to do. A panicked amygdala is not always helpful – unless you need a huge shot of adrenaline to turbo-swim away from a shark, for example! This neurological relationship between stress and your breath is central. And we know that being in water regulates your breath, and therefore automatically helps to improve your stress levels. Simple neuroscience.

Bluespace, Nature and Wellbeing

Research that I will talk about in more detail later in this chapter shows us that being in nature and by water improves our wellbeing; and the concept of 'Blue Mind', as we've heard, refers to the healing effects of looking at, being next to, or in water. I know that for me and many of my friends, there is little that cannot be cured, or at least forgotten about temporarily, by throwing yourself into cold seawater. Many a day, after a particularly hideous London commute, I've almost sprinted to the sea – an almost desperate need for physical and psychological relief after a bad day. I'm sure some of you can relate to this.

Why should this be so? Well, green and bluespaces (i.e. nature and water) help to regulate the activity of the anxiety/panic centres, the amygdalae in the brain. It's been proved that being in or next to these spaces reduces stress levels and improves our mood, our physical fitness and even our self-esteem. These nature experiences all help to regulate the activity of the amygdalae in the brain. Even if you don't live near the sea, you can find your own form of water, such as a pond, lake, canal, river, a relaxing bath or even a cold shower. All help to energise your body and calm your mind. The rest of this book will show us how to do this – and the benefits it brings to our bodies, minds and communities.

Bluespace refers simply to 'all surface waters' in nature (see Volker and Kistemann's work on this).[5] So this means oceans, seas, rivers, lakes, ponds and waterfalls. If we want to, we can add a human dimension and include fountains, garden water features, and even indoor baths and showers. All give us views of, or offer immersion in, water. Academics are starting to look hard at the evidence around how bluespace relates to our wellbeing. As mentioned earlier, there are different ways of 'doing research' into wellbeing. Objective (or positivist) research tends to use large samples of people, experiments or surveys with closed questions that can later be tested. This way of doing things is important as when a study is carried out in this way, the results can predict with a fair degree of certainty that their findings hold true across large populations and in most cases. This 'evidence-based research' is preferred for medical and health/science studies.

Subjective or interpretivist approaches to research allow for a more individual perspective on any topic, such as how people feel about things, how they experience them, their behaviours and personal attitudes. This is my own preferred approach to research. But what we are seeing in the area of bluespace and wellbeing is the need for *both* approaches to come together. While many of us know that water helps us to feel well (it is something very intuitive or 'felt'), in order for public health programmes to encourage this approach, we need more scientific 'evidence' to back it up. There are small stirrings of this work being done here in the UK and also in the US. The National Health Service in Cornwall, for example, is now prescribing water-activities for certain health conditions.[6] The Wave Project is a charitable organisation originating there that takes young people with specific health conditions into the sea to teach them to surf, often on specially adapted surfboards. [7] It has proved hugely popular and a lifeline to many who would not otherwise be able to access the sea.

If we can gather enough information across a wide range of study-types, then our future health systems may well look very different to the medication-heavy protocols we now have. The coronavirus pandemic of 2020 shone a very bright, insightful light on how much humans *really value* nature and water. They took their small allowances of outdoor engagement to their hearts and minds, and for many this green and blue nature was a mental-health lifebuoy. A profound hiatus in many ways.

Beginnings

Let's go back a bit first. This attraction to the water is not new, nor is it confined to any one culture. There is a long history of folk attachment to 'healing water places' in many countries. The 'holy well', for example, is a mythical place in many rural areas in the UK and Ireland, where people have traditionally gone for cures for various physical conditions (see Ronan Foley's work for more on holy wells). [8, 9] I remember my own grandmother marching us all down as kids to St Mogue's Well in Clonmore, Ireland, to dip our primary-school, wart-ridden fingers into its mysterious waters! Even the Christian faith in 'holy water' is interesting to contemplate – a font stands by the door of each church. One of my favourite images of the 2020 coronavirus social-distancing regime was that of a priest doing a drive-through church service, where he shot holy water from a water-pistol through the open windows of parishioners' car windows as they passed by. Divine relief perhaps?

The religious and folk attraction of water is seen in other places too, such as Lourdes in France, and indeed many places where pilgrimages of faith take place. Water is seen as a purifier in many religions.

Eastern Europe also has a long tradition of high-mineral-based *terme*, or spa waters. Many still go to these sites for arthritic or orthopaedic relief, as people have done for centuries. The Japanese *onsen* give relief to many; as a volcanic island, Japan is littered with these hot-spring sites, and there are whole cultural traditions and rituals associated with them. The ancient Romans and Greeks similarly had elaborate baths and bathing houses, and they spread these traditions across the European continent. Today, Turkish baths remain popular both inside and outside Turkey itself. In Scandinavia, the combination of hot sauna and ice-lake dipping is another long-standing tradition. There isn't time here to cover the whole history of water and cultural traditions, but suffice to say water has always been, and still remains, hugely important to us as human beings in very many different ways.

Bluespace Wellbeing Impacts

I think what's interesting to note about both the history of water in society and current research studies of water is the range of wellbeing outcomes we can consider. For some people, there is very real physical relief that comes with being in water. On a trip to Hungary some years ago, I noticed with surprise the high percentage of very elderly people at a famous spa I visited with a friend. I later found out that there was an orthopaedic hospital attached to the spa hotel. For other people, there is an immensely positive social-wellbeing aspect to connecting with others in the water. And for many more, there is the psychological wellbeing improvement that comes with being next to, looking at or being immersed in water – in all its forms. Let's look at a sample of the work that's been carried out around these themes.

Research is beginning to confirm that wellbeing improvement can be directly related to being near (either living or visiting) the sea, or partaking in activities in or by the sea. As a growing body of evidence is showing, humans place high emotional value on coastal places and experiences for themselves, their families and their psychological health. In this respect, Wil Gesler's findings on 'therapeutic landscapes' are outstanding.[10, 11] Gesler is an American medical geography professor (yes, there is such a thing – think: place meets health!). He has worked in Africa and the US, researching how we think about and practise health and wellbeing. In his book *Health Places*, for example, he asks if there can be 'healing beyond the walls of a modern hospital'. He examines how different environments affect our physical, mental, spiritual, social and emotional healing, and sets out four dimensions found in healing environments: natural, built, symbolic and social. In particular, he looks at landscapes where physical and built environments, social conditions and human perceptions combine to produce an atmosphere which is conducive to healing or wellbeing. His ideas on natural places as 'therapeutic landscapes' was really ground-breaking in its simplicity! The notion that certain places make us feel better is something many of us know, intuitively. I definitely like to think of all watery bluespaces as therapeutic landscapes!

Other social science research focuses on quantitative reviews of bluespace health and wellbeing,[12] while others assess more intangible concepts of the relationship between place and happiness. A key question is: how do people value water for their own wellbeing?

A University of Exeter study by Dr Matthew White and his interdisciplinary team looked at 'monitoring engagement with the natural environment'.[13] White is an environmental psychologist with an interest in natural environments, human health and wellbeing, and pro-environmental behaviour and wellbeing. He is also a surfer, living in Cornwall (not jealous at all, nope!). Exeter's research data interestingly showed that everyday visits to the coast were associated with higher levels of stress-reducing positive emotions (e.g. calmness, relaxation and revitalisation) than visits to urban parks or open countryside. So bluespace trumps greenspace, the research shows! Data collected from two large, nationally representative surveys of leisure visits to the English coast also suggest that a sense of restoration and stress reduction are integral to what's known as a 'healthy coast effect'. [14] Further research at Portsmouth University by Heather Massey and Mike Tipton et al. refers to 'health by stealth' near water.[15] So, in other words, without really trying too hard, we improve our physical and mental wellbeing (including treating depression) through engagement with water.

Research also shows us that bluespaces frequently feature among people's favourite places to *visit* for restoration and relaxation. Some of the UK's well-loved watery places therefore have the power to create positive wellbeing through memory, recall, return visits and more. I think we can all easily call to mind favourite family trips to the sea, lakes or rivers. So, in many ways water offers a unique temporal or time-spectrum experience too: the wellbeing power of now, as we engage with it in the moment (e.g. today's swim high or walk by the river), and also the wellbeing power of the past (such as a favourite holiday or moment by the water) as we *remember* it. I also think time spent too far away from the water creates a yearning for it in many people – a longing for a trip to the sea or the lake. I remember speaking at a conference in land-locked Austria a few years ago, slightly feeling like Chicken Licken from the fairy tale – the sky closing in on me over the towering, snow-peaked mountains. When I returned to Brighton, I needed to get to the seafront immediately, to see the horizon and throw myself into the water. For many people who don't live by the sea, this feeling comes up when they go on holiday. Remember that feeling, almost tripping on your own clothes as children (or even adults!) in a rush to get undressed, into your swimming costume and dash for the waves?

To understand conceptually a little more about why wellbeing and water are closely connected, we can look at a few interesting concepts briefly:

1) place attachment;
2) emotional geographies and environmental connectedness; and
3) therapeutic landscapes theory.

These are not quantitative measures, but they do help us to *understand* things more deeply.

Place Attachment

Place attachment can be described as an emotional bond or positive connection between an individual and a particular place. We can see this, for example, when we talk about our favourite beach, or our favourite spot to sit by the lake. I spoke in Chapter 1 about the west coast of Mayo being my 'soul landscape'; this is in essence, place attachment. I can recall instantly, in my mind's eye, the rock I used to sit on at 'my beach' there, or the way the sand looks and feels on Crantock Beach in Cornwall, where I go on holiday with my family each year. I'm sure you have your own special places near water. Are they in your life every day, places from the past, or just at holiday times? Why do they matter so much to us? Why do we go back to them?

Place attachment can be further divided into sub categories: 'place identity', where a place has symbolic importance as a repository for emotions (such as a place where we can feel well and be ourselves – for many of us, this is in the water!) and relationships that give meaning to human life; and 'place dependence', which refers to how places provide the conditions that facilitate people's goals in life (e.g., the idea that we can live well here). Both aspects of place attachment, simply framed, are considered important in individual wellbeing and in the notion of custodianship for the natural environment. Arguably, feeling physically and emotionally well due to perceived benefits of bluespace engagement increases our levels of place attachment. In other words, if a place makes us feel good, we feel part of that place somehow, and that matters to us.

Emotional Geographies and Environmental Connectedness

From the field of environmental psychology, the concept of 'environmental-connectedness' emphasises the transformative power of nature experiences and encounters.[17] Your first winter of cold water swimming can change your whole experience of your own body and mind. By regular immersion, you may feel a profound connection to the water that you perhaps took for granted before. Maybe you just walked next to it, but didn't consider getting into it. I know that since I began to swim all year round in cold water, I now find it hard to pass any body of water, anywhere, anytime, without thinking to myself, 'I wonder if I could get into that?' This immersion deepens our connection to our bluespace environments. When we feel more connected to our watery environment I think we are more likely to look after it. These protectionist emotions are rooted in our own improved felt-wellbeing, personal values, positive emotions and memory making.

Emotional connections with the natural environment can also be explained through the concept of 'lived space', i.e. the relationships between people and settings that are generated *in place*, and the emotions that thus emerge through participation in or inhabitation of our bluespace world. [18] The term 'emotional geographies' captures a sense of how certain places make us feel, and how we then might respond to them. I think it is a lovely way of thinking about things.

Because of its wild beauty and the sensory nature of water itself (whether this takes the form of expansive vistas, sea salt, wind, the roar or lapping of the waves, or the flow of running river water), it is often observed that water has the power to produce a sense of awe, or perspective, in the human individual. In using the word 'produce', it can be further argued that our seas, lakes, rivers and oceans have a capacity to *generate and sustain* emotional connections and therefore have some kind of proactive 'agency', rather than just being backdrops to our lives.

We can experience very keenly this relationship between ourselves and our environment through bluespace walks or swims. These can generate psychological wellbeing despite the details of weather or other conditions. Research from Bondi Beach Australia, for example, showed the high value respondents placed on their daily beach practices (such as walking or surfing) in a space often exposed to natural extremes (including winds and large waves) as well as human overcrowding, yet which still generated tranquil and happy emotions. [19] Therefore, these theories around place attachment, environmental-connectedness and emotions serve, I think, as strong foundations for considering the sense of wellbeing that comes from bluespace engagement for many of us.

Therapeutic Landscapes

Human beings have long sought out water for solace, stillness and rehabilitation, and the concept of therapeutic landscapes (those places that geographer Will Gesler refers to which heal us or offer improved physical and psychological wellbeing) is really interesting. According to attention restoration theory (ART), natural settings are rich in features that enhance mental functioning. The coast and its waters can thus literally help to 'restore our attention' or ability to function and focus and be present in our daily lives... and therefore to feel *well*. This psycho-evolutionary model suggests also that natural environments enable *recovery from* any form of stress, not just attention restoration.

Sarah Bell and her team at the University of Exeter medical school present a useful model (see page 38) that summarises the therapeutic landscape experience 'dimensions' we can engage with at the coast, and how they make us feel well in different ways.[20] Bell is a lecturer in health geography, whose research explores the role of everyday 'nature' encounters in shaping experiences of health, wellbeing, mobility and disability through our life course.

This model basically shows us how and why coastal spaces are experienced as 'therapeutic' (therefore increasing our wellbeing) by highlighting the links between bluespace, health and wellbeing. Emotional attachments to the coast can develop through the accumulation of diverse individual and/or shared coastal experiences. The research of Bell and her colleagues has shown that some people prioritise opportunities to use the coast to progress towards personal goals or ('achieving' experiences), such as running, walking, even distance swimming or other sports-related actions; while others value opportunities to lose themselves ('immersive' experiences) or connect with others ('social' experiences). Several participants in a study of coastal wellbeing in southwest England valued experiences of 'immersive *restoration*' at the coast, where they reported lower levels of stress and better mood.[21] ART theory has been widely studied in the context of green nature spaces but only recently in relation to bluespace. I think it has great value in terms of a way of thinking about the benefits of water for wellbeing.

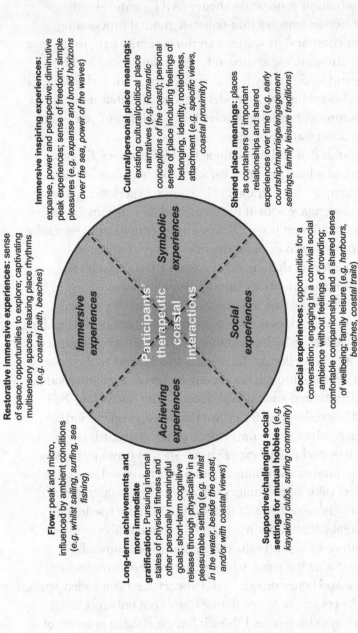

Immersive inspiring experiences: expanse, power and perspective; diminutive peak experiences; sense of freedom; simple pleasures (e.g. expanse and broad horizons over the sea, power of the waves)

Cultural/personal place meanings: existing cultural/political place narratives (e.g. Romantic conceptions of the coast); personal sense of place including feelings of belonging, identity, rootedness, attachment (e.g. specific views, coastal proximity)

Shared place meanings: places as containers of important relationships and shared experiences over time (e.g. early courtship/marriage/engagement settings, family leisure traditions)

Restorative immersive experiences: sense of space; opportunities to explore; captivating multisensory spaces; relaxing place rhythms (e.g. coastal path, beaches)

Flow: peak and micro, influenced by ambient conditions (e.g. whilst sailing, surfing, sea fishing)

Long-term achievements and more immediate gratification: Pursuing internal states of physical fitness and other personally meaningful goals; short-term cognitive release through physicality in a pleasurable setting (e.g. whilst in the water, beside the coast, and/or with coastal views)

Supportive/challenging social settings for mutual hobbies (e.g. kayaking clubs, surfing community)

Social experiences: opportunities for a conversation; engaging in a convivial social ambience without feelings of crowding; comfortable companionship and a shared sense of wellbeing; family leisure (e.g. harbours, beaches, coastal trails)

Symbolic experiences

Immersive experiences

Participants' therapeutic coastal interactions

Social experiences

Achieving experiences

Therapeutic coastal interactions
Bell et al (2015)[20]

Overall, as an academic who swims, writes, teaches and is a wellbeing practitioner too, I find depth and intellectual curiosity in thinking about how we can explain these intricate relationships between water and wellbeing.[22] Place, water, time, bluespace, memory, meaning, connection and wellbeing are so finely intertwined.

The Effects of Water on Our Wellbeing

So, we've had a look at some of the research on bluespaces, water and wellbeing. We can think next about what research says about *the effects* water has on our physical wellbeing, our mental wellbeing and our social wellbeing. Let's begin with the physical.

Water and Physical Wellbeing

Lots of interesting work is starting to emerge across many fields relating to cold water science, the physical body and wellbeing. In particular, research is looking at the possible links between cold water swimming and reduced levels of depression, anxiety and the control of inflammation. Some of the main areas of interest include research undertaken by Dr Mark Harper, a cardiac anaesthetist based in Sussex. Mark is an enthusiastic converted cold water swimmer – like many of us!

In an interview, 'The Healing Madness of Sea Swimming', he talks about research into several key areas on cold water and wellbeing.[23] He begins by stating that depression and inflammation in the body are closely linked. You can, he says, treat depression to a certain extent by giving anti-inflammatory drugs. We also know that when our bodies get used to swimming in cold open water, 'cold water adaptation' happens: the practice reduces levels of inflammation. Even putting just your face into cold water stimulates your parasympathetic nervous system (see page 26) and *that* has an anti-inflammatory effect as well.

So how do you get cold water adapted? Harper notes that when we first get into cold water, before we become adapted to it, our heart rate increases, we can't control our breathing and we may hyperventilate, which feels, to all intents and purposes, like a panic attack. This is absolutely normal! The way you know you're starting to adapt is when you stay in the water just long enough to get your breathing under control. At that point, you've done all you need to do for the process of adaptation, for that single swim. Within approximately six swims (at 14°C), you will be adapted to cold water. He suggests beginning in the summer seas or in freshwater and building up gradually.

As well as reducing inflammation in the body, cold water swimming helps in other ways too. Chronic stress situations in our daily lives (such as rushing for trains, juggling childcare and work, and so on) create what Harper calls 'a surge of stress'. This triggers our sympathetic nervous system (see page 26). But when we are adapted to cold water, this surge of stress will be a *lower* surge. Therefore, cold water swimming in natural bluespaces reduces our stress response overall.

Harper worked with the BBC on a programme called *The Doctor who Gave up Drugs*, in which a 24-year-old female volunteer, who had suffered with chronic depression since the age of 16, took part in a programme of cold water adaptation to see if it would help her.[24] She had been taking antidepressants for eight years. On the first day, she was asked to take four cold water baths in the research lab. Her low mood almost prevented her from completing the task, but she did and by the fourth dip there was a boost to her feelings. The next day, the team took her to a lake for some cold water swimming. Before their eyes, she changed from withdrawn to 'happy, smiley and buzzy', according to

Harper. She spoke of her sense of achievement – and this is important too, in terms of increasing our wellbeing – in having overcome something difficult. Four months later, and still consistently swimming outdoors, she was doing well and still off all antidepressants.

Cold water swimming can therefore help with many stress-related conditions such as anxiety and depression – or any inflammation-related conditions in the body. I think that is pretty amazing, and really look forward to more research evidence on this. Imagine if our bluespaces in nature held the key to our health and wellbeing all along? Incredible!

As I mentioned earlier, a combination of scientific/objective and subjective research approaches is critical in providing a full picture of how and why water makes us feel well. I recently sat on a panel at a sold-out public symposium for blue health, where Dr Mark Harper spoke about the physical benefits of cold water swimming, an NHS psychologist spoke about its mental health benefits and I was able to talk about the wider bluespace contexts and the importance of social wellbeing access, and connection. It was the perfect cocktail! It is this kind of joined-up thinking and collaborative research that I believe will make a huge impact as we move forward in promoting blue health as a 'natural prescription' for wellbeing.

Another cold water enthusiast with growing credence is Wim Hof, fondly known as 'the Iceman'. He has brought the physicality of cold water benefits to many people. This Dutchman (who holds *The Guinness Book of Records* title for the longest swim under ice) has a large and loyal following for his 'Wim Hof Method'.[25] His method, based on his own scientific research, has three main pillars built around the relationship between water and wellbeing:

- cold therapy (the bluespace doesn't have to be the sea or a lake, but can be a bucket of ice water or a cold shower);

- breathing (to reduce stress and boost the immune system – see the earlier section on Stress, on page 25);
- commitment (needed to move out of our own comfort zones, especially around cold temperatures).

His way into physical (and indeed mental) wellbeing comes from what he calls 'cold hard nature'. It is not for everyone, but it has grown in popularity and the feedback is mainly very positive.

There are many terms used to talk about how water can help our physical wellbeing. 'BlueGym' was a 2009 initiative in the UK (led by Dr Matthew White again, at Exeter University) created to explore whether the sea and coastal environments can have positive effects on health and wellbeing, particularly by increasing physical exercise and exposure to vitamin D. [26] Overall, we can say that water does indeed improve our physical wellbeing. Rather than paying to go inside to an artificial gym environment of treadmills and rowing machines, we can walk and run alongside moving water, or row a real boat in natural surroundings, breathing in fresh oxygen and allowing our bodies to connect to the earth and water around us. When we increase our heart rate through physical activity next to, on, or in the water, this in turn improves our physical fitness, our cardiac health, our weight and respiration levels. So, physically, bluespaces are very conducive to improved physical wellbeing. But we need to *want* to go into water, and we need to be psychologically and emotionally *able* to feel the benefits.

Water and Psychological Wellbeing

One of the most common things anyone who cold water swims all year without a wetsuit is asked is: 'WHY would you do that to yourself?' The very simple answer for many of us is … 'Because it makes me feel good.' Even in the cold winter? Yes, especially then. The cold water high we mentioned earlier is the perfect example of the body–mind relationship. The vagus nerve boost we get and the endorphins that are released through cold water swimming improve our mood, as simple as that. Cold water stimulates the vagus nerve, which runs from the neck to the abdomen and is in charge of turning off the 'fight, flight or freeze' panic reflex. The vagus nerve activates your relaxation response, reducing your heart rate and blood pressure. The deep breathing we need to do when we get into cold water in particular, turns on the vagus nerve so that it acts as a brake on the stress response. This also explains why mindful meditation deep breathing makes us feel calm pretty much instantly.

Some of the studies I've conducted myself look at the positive mental health aspects of bluespace engagement. There are those people who find it hard to put a finger on what it is exactly that makes them feel better, while others are very clear: 'I don't know what it is really, I just cheer up when I see the sea,' an outdoor swimmer told me. Another fervently believes that 'throwing myself into the sea just clears my brain, it literally washes out all the crap from my head – just like that. Nothing else in the world does that for me so easily and without effort.'

For many bluespace enthusiasts, though, a regular practice of swimming or even visits to water soon builds up a dependency on it. Many people in various surveys soon find that they don't quite feel themselves if they don't go as often as they would like. Many feel that their wellbeing suffers, especially their mental wellbeing:

> *I like being immersed in nature and the changing landscape around you. The reset, clear-your-head-of-anything-else feeling, whilst you're swimming (especially so in the winter). Being held by the water – I still find this kind of magical and spiritual.*

This healing reset is a practical tool for some, but for others the water is a way to manage chronic pain in a joyful way:

Sea swimming has become coping a mechanism for chronic pain and the mental stress that goes along with that. It's the ultimate form of mindfulness: every sense is engaged so you can't think, only feel. Also, it's the camaraderie and support of my swim pals and the well-deserved post-swim coffee and cake with lots of laughs.

We can see again here the many different aspects that can make up an individual's personal sense of wellbeing. It's what happens in our minds when we are in bluespace that is critical.

Blue Mind

Wallace J. Nichols' seminal book *Blue Mind* has been a game-changing work for many.[27] It brought to the public a way of talking about our love of the seas and oceans that many of us knew to be true, but hadn't quite connected to our state of mind, or in terms of its connections to others and ourselves. I love this book for many reasons! Nichols explains how 'being in, on, or under water can make you happier, healthier, more connected and better at what you do'. Nichols is an American marine biologist who mixes his expertise in the science of the oceans with his love and passion for them. He writes with enthusiasm about the many benefits bluespace can bring to the human mind, economy and overall wellbeing.

Without trying to summarise the whole book here (though do read it, it's wonderful!), some of the main points to take away are explanations of how water calms our brain, creating a state of 'drift' where our mental attention is not forced or directed, but rather is involuntary and therefore more peaceful. This is supported by environmental psychologists Kaplan and Kaplan, who have studied the effects of bluespace on the brain and our moods.[28] For Nichols, drift is an important element of Blue Mind. It is, he says, a state of calm – where water engagement reduces our blood pressure and decreases stress hormones and the activity of the sympathetic (emergency) nervous system.

What I also like about Nichols' work is that he too enjoys presenting a mix of the scientific and the personal, the spiritual even.[29] I think that's important if we are to take on board the idea that wellbeing really is about a balance between body, mind and spirit, or soul, or whatever term you fancy for that 'other' existential part of ourselves. The tone of his book is very much Californian surf mood, and it makes me want to go hang out there and retire – but he is nicely irreverent about that too. There can be, in the self-help and wellbeing area, a tendency towards being slightly 'worthy' and adopting the serious, spiritual vibes of the evangelical; this can be true, for example, of those who promote vigilant, committed practice of various types of meditation, yoga, or the latest neurolinguistic 'thing'. Water, Nichols declares with simple glee, meditates *you*! Brilliant. And it does.

There is a lovely phrase the Japanese use called 'living water', which means that we humans pour some of ourselves into the water when we get into it. It in turn somehow takes our emotions and reconfigures them; it takes our physical aches and our mental anguish, and soothes and calms them. In this way, the water is not just alive with its own wildlife and vegetation, it is alive with us and our emotions. This is certainly what I have felt in my own grief, as I described in Chapter 1.

These emotional geographies of living water feel very real. The idea I mentioned in my own research about water having 'agency' comes up again here in this sense. Water and bluespace, I'd argue, are more than just a neutral and benign backdrop for us to exercise in, like some kind of bland gym. It does *so* much more for us than that. This living water is something we enter into a relationship with when we go to it.

While Blue Mind is a state of positive mental being, Nichols speaks of the opposite state, 'red mind' – where we are stressed, our bodies and minds inflamed, busy, rushing, worried, forward-thinking and anxious. He prescribes water as a solution. This Blue Mind state of calm is something that water does for us; it changes the neurological patterns in our brain. And as we saw earlier, it incites physiological changes in our bodies. Beyond all of that, many of us experience a state of bliss, calm, peace, or, in very cold water, a 'high' after we get out. The latter gives us a clear mind, where we can then go on to be productive in a very focused way, he suggests. Therein lies the benefit of an early morning swim, for those who can get to it!

Psychological Non-Wellbeing

For many people, today's world is not slow enough, not kind enough and not forgiving enough – of body shapes, of mental states and of different ways of being. Many of us suffer from the effects of constant stress, others from severe trauma, and more still from diagnosed mental health issues. There has been a rising scientific interest in whether open water swimming might have clinical value, especially for those suffering with depression. The results are promising, as we saw earlier with Dr Mark Harper's collaborative research.

Hannah Denton, a UK clinical psychologist and open swimmer herself, undertook an empirical study in which she innovatively interviewed people whilst *in* the water, as well as through land-based surveys. [30] Her work showed three important dimensions of bluespace swimming: transformation, connection and reorientation. The respondents in her research talked about how their mood could change during the course of a swim and afterwards, using words such as 'healing' and a 'way to escape'. Secondly, they spoke of connection and belonging. Her respondents were part of an open water swimming club in this instance

– so they spoke of connecting to the natural watery world, but also to each other. The third aspect of this work is where people speak about how the sea gives them a new perspective on their day – a 'reorientation,' Denton calls it. For many of us, a bad morning or a bad day can temporarily be reset by getting into the water. All three of these dimensions improve our wellbeing, Denton observes, and asks: 'Is it time to revisit the sea cure?'

Some of the people I have spoken to feel strongly that cold water swimming has changed their relationship with their mental ill health, and has even prevented hospitalisation. The pandemic of 2020, which stopped people from accessing cold water for several months, took its toll very badly on those who had come to depend on it to keep psychologically well. A respondent to my survey on this noted: 'I miss the way it silences the stress in my brain and stops my autistic meltdowns. *Like a prescription missed*, I crave the relief it brings.' I think this is a hugely powerful metaphor, don't you?

One of the things antidepressant drugs do is regulate our mood through (among other things) the stimulation of the vagus nerve. Cold water immersion, however, especially of the face and neck, stimulates this nerve naturally! Pharmaceutical companies try to emulate this effect in their drug production. This shows us again the great potential power that water holds for mental health interventions, and the close relationship between mind, body and nature. Or, as some of my sea-swimming friends like to shout in the heart of winter as we stick our faces into freezing water, 'Vagus, baby!'

Water and Social Wellbeing

Speaking of friends, this brings me to the final jigsaw piece I want to talk about in terms of wellbeing. Social wellbeing is encapsulated in the term 'community'. The term *connect* is one of the Five Ways to Wellbeing, and this is no accident. For many who reap the benefits of bluespace wellbeing, it is all about connecting with other people at or in the water. This makes us feel well – the idea that we have a social world.

Open water swimming creates a sense of community, even if it is a temporary one, with a very specific shared purpose. Hannah Denton's work verified this from a clinical point of view. And my own research into how people, particularly families, connect better to each other in bluespaces also supports this idea of how water helps to join people together, often in the 'best versions' of themselves. Community is an essential part of the concept of wellbeing and social sciences research tells us that it is a vital part of our overall health.

Loneliness and isolation are common ills in modern society. Many people do not know their neighbours nor feel part of the place they live in. I spoke earlier about the idea of 'place attachment' – and that is something the water offers us. And for many of us, along with this comes the offering of the loveliest swimming communities you can imagine… When I asked people how much water meant to them, this idea of swimming 'together' ranked very highly. One interviewee told me: 'Cold water swimming helps with my anxiety, it soothes me to get a saltwater rush on my skin and has introduced me to some of the greatest friendships of my life…'

What is somewhat unusual in many wild swimming groups is the uniqueness of the community. Unlike other communities, which are often linked by shared living or work spaces, outdoor swimmers don't necessarily know each other in any deep way. There are very few conversations about what anyone does for a living, families, places of residence, or the other markers that often select friendship groupings. Instead, there is common sense of a love for the water that simply, and effectively, joins people together. Community, as Dr Mark Harper notes, is what 'keeps you going'. Others in a swim community support each other and make you more likely to keep at it – which is why bluespace swimming is more likely to keep you well, for longer!

There is often a huge sense of play, of fun and much laughter – unlike in almost any other adult group. The water allows us to be, feel, and act young – regardless of our age. And that too, research shows us, is very good for our mental health. It is neurologically impossible to be anxious at the same time as we are laughing! As one Brighton sea swimmer said aptly, 'I was thinking about the permission the sea gives us to play. To jump, to whoop, to dance in the waves. Try and second-guess its force and movement and then collapse into its arms. Full embodiment of emotions.'

I think one of the most important things this new surge of 'wild swimming' groups has done (besides reaping the physical benefits of water), is to allow *access* to the sea, lakes and other bluespaces like never before. That and the ease of social media. Many groups are self-regulating – someone posts a suggestion of a time or place they are free to swim, and whoever fancies it can join in. The groups are welcoming, friendly and encouraging. It takes great courage for many people to show up and join in anything, especially without the support framework of work or perhaps school connections. I have seen so many tentative posts from women (usually) saying they are new to all this, and looking for advice on what to wear and when to go, etc. – met with gentle, positive and joyful offers of support. The 'social capital' needed to be brave enough to reply to a text can be more than some people have, however. I live in Hove, a well-to-do part of the city of Brighton, on the south coast of England (an hour from London) where there are lots of well-educated, privileged people who can work flexibly (I count myself among these) – but not everyone falls into this category.

One of the loveliest things I've seen in this respect has been the instigation of an 'access to water and wellbeing' course for women, set up by the Brighton 'Salty Seabirds' social enterprise, which I mentioned in Chapter 1. The Seabirds were founded to bring salty wellbeing to people through sea swimming, confidence building and learning. Their women's access course was funded with grant aid, so it was free to participants. The course allowed attendees from women's refuges, or those with mental wellbeing challenges, to come along and get a taste of watery wellness in a safe, supported and friendly environment.

A Seabirds' pilot study first asked people about the fears they had of going into the sea. Common worries were of not being a good enough or 'proper' swimmer, not understanding tides or rip currents, body-exposure, and a fear of going into the water alone. The courses have been, to my mind, a benchmark of good practice that many bluespace communities could follow. They comprised experienced swimmer instructors, volunteer support helpers (of all shapes and sizes, to de-mystify the notion of the perfect beach body) and kind, supportive fun. There was a mix of conversation, learning, and the creation of a safe, held, watery space where some of those most in need could let the sea work its magic. I think we could all do more to create these opportunities so that everyone in society can access the benefits of bluespace wellbeing. This is a practical mission I want to work on personally.

The last aspect of social wellbeing I want to talk about relates to my own research on families, children, and social connections at the water.[31] I've looked at how going to the sea in particular helps to create memorable experiences that form an important part of family memories, stories and legacies. In my own family, and I'm sure in many of yours, the sea is central to most of our much-loved holidays and day trips. In the depths of winter, or on a rainy day, we often talk about 'Do you remember the time in Cornwall when… or that day we surfed in Portugal…' and it keeps us going.

The other interesting aspect of social wellbeing that I found in my research is that bluespace really helps to bond families, and bring out their own authentic sense of themselves. There is a sense, somehow, of 'being a proper family' – of being a good dad or a good mum – that the beach and sea facilitates. At an individual level, as mentioned earlier, many swimmers have talked about being able to 'be my real self' at or in the water. This is known as 'existential authenticity', this idea of being our real selves, individually, or in the roles we play in our families.

I find it fascinating to think about how and why many people feel that bluespace is where proper 'quality time' happens – a place where meaningful interactions take place. As if, somehow, our busy everyday stressful lives can become suspended, and we present the better versions of ourselves. This is what lots of social research tells us about the important role of holidays, but I've found that bluespace does the same job, whether on holiday or not. One of my research respondents observed:

> *When we are all here, I really see my kids – notice them, you know? I appreciate them all over again. Just playing, covered in ice cream or whatever, being themselves. And I look at my husband and remember how lucky we are to have them, and each other I suppose. This is what it's all about, isn't it?*

For many families, the sea is central in their holiday imaginations and memories. 'I can't imagine us going on any holiday that isn't by the sea,' one parent told me. 'It's what we do, and what we've always done.' So, the stories we create at the water become an important part of our family identity, and of our individual identity too, I think. We construct ideas of 'who we are' in bluespaces: a family who surfs, a couple who wakeboard, cousins who camp at the lake, a woman who swims all year, and so on. These quality times and connections with water, and with each other, allow us to cope with our everyday worlds and create a *stronger sense of ourselves*.

Blue Soul

I'm wondering, as I conclude this chapter, if there is scope to talk about how all these aspects of wellbeing come together for some people. A 'blue soul' of sorts? For me, even reading the words 'bluespace, Blue Mind, blue soul' makes me feel calm and centred. In my mind's eye when I read them, I can see turquoise and blue-green waters, calm and crashing waves, sparkling freshwater and flowing rivers. I can feel the cold water, hear the *shush* of the waves brushing up and down a pebble beach, inhale the smell of the salt... and my mind settles. With these visuals and these sensory stimuli, I come home to myself in a way that is hard to put into words.

There are days when the water makes me feel physically fit and well, present in my body – and others when it soothes my busy, tired brain. But collectively, bluespace helps me to feel more at peace with myself, with my own spirit, in the gentlest sense of the word. Blue soul is a coming together of all these facets of wellbeing that research continues to investigate, yet it is not something at all tangible or quantifiable. It is just beyond our explanatory reach – an intuitive and internal homecoming offered by these spaces, which we love, value and need.

3

BLUESPACE WELLBEING:
PRINCIPLES AND PRACTICES

We saw in the last chapter how bluespaces are talked about in scientific research and other writings. What I'd like to do now is think about how bluespaces are *experienced* in ways that makes us *feel* well. One of the things that came up in Chapter 2 was that wellbeing means different things to different people. This subjectivity is important, because it means one size does not fit all. I have a friend, for example, who hates meditation – can't do it, won't do it and it holds little appeal for her. The same woman can power through deep water like a fish, dive off cliffs and handle a surfboard with ease. For some of us, wellbeing can be found through doing or moving; for others, the quest for calm is of the essence. Whatever your preference, water has it all, whether you are in it, on it or beside it.

Let's examine some of the ways *into* bluespace wellbeing now. I want to think about these different ways that water makes us feel better and will be sharing some practical exercises, case studies and personal stories. However, any exercises suggested here should be undertaken only within your own comfort zone and ability levels, so please go gently and listen to your own body and mind.

Being

In the fast-paced world many of us inhabit, there is implicit value placed on achievement and productivity. We greet each other at the school gates or at home with 'What did you do today?' enquiries, and often, our evaluation of our day depends on how much we 'got done'. I hear friends sadly self-remonstrate with, 'Oh, I didn't get a lot done today' as they then list various childcare duties and hidden domestic chores they've accomplished. Or, for some, depression, family problems, perimenopause symptoms of fatigue and low mood, or a host of other conditions can stop us from doing what we and others expect of us. There is almost a fear around 'not doing enough', as if our life were being graded against some imaginary checklist that we need to tick off each day, each week or each year.

Why do we do this to ourselves? Well, mainly because we are conditioned to. Our school systems begin at a very young age with 'targets' and assessments around a set of 'doing' skills. We are compared to each other competitively all the way through childhood until our early twenties in a cold and judgemental way, on a very narrow range of abilities. One thing that tends to be overlooked in these skewed structures we have set ourselves is the need to 'just be'. The ability to 'be' simply means the ability to be still and quiet within our minds. An intention, if you like, to not constantly *react* to everything, every person, every situation with judgement. When we do that, we become exhausted and stressed very quickly. It's as if there is no 'off switch' in our bodies and minds, except when we sleep.

Those of us who use bluespaces know that water helps us switch off our minds and bodies from everyday stresses – and we can combine this elemental force of nature with other strategies too, to improve our wellbeing even more deeply. Let's think about this state of 'being', or 'being present' for a minute. In essence, this is mindfulness, or very simply, bringing our mind into focus, almost like a camera lens, as we try to hold our attention and breath on what we are doing. I'd like to consider next what mindfulness is and how the principles at its heart can help us in our everyday lives – especially when we are in bluespace.

What is Mindfulness?

I have practised and dipped into many forms of physical, spiritual and psychological wellbeing over the last two decades. For me, however, mindfulness is something that just clicked many elements into place in a very simple, effective and practical way. Practising mindfulness is a way of thinking, being and engaging in your own world that helps you move through it in a way that is calmer for you.

There are many definitions and approaches to mindfulness, and it is rolled out now in many contexts as the cure for everything under the sun, but don't let that put you off. I like to use Jon Kabat-Zinn's work – the Harvard doctor who developed the acclaimed MBSR (mindfulness-based stress reduction) programme – as the now go-to, non-drug option for helping with stress and anxiety. His key book *Full Catastrophe Living* is an important foundation for any understanding of mindfulness and its practice. [1] Simply put, mindfulness is *'moment by moment, non-judgemental awareness'*. This sounds pretty simple, but in essence, it is hard to achieve without lots of practice.

We can talk about different ways of understanding mindfulness, including 'just being here now', or deliberately noticing how we are thinking and feeling, in this moment, without having unhelpful judgemental opinions about ourselves, others, or the activity/situation we are in. We can consider the key aspects of mindfulness and understand how they might be applied to different bluespace settings.

The Basic Principles of Mindfulness

A starting point for delving into mindfulness is to reflect for a minute on how much of our own lives are lived on autopilot. Like that moment where you arrive at the end of your car or train journey, and know that you have arrived, but aren't quite sure how you got there? Or when you find yourself replaying in your mind the dialogue of an argument with a spouse, or conflict with a child or colleague; or that mental ticker-tape of running-commentary worries around the tasks you must face this week, as you munch your granola with an acid stomach – all taking up space in your mind, and allowing the here-and-now to be relegated somewhere else.

If our mind is preoccupied with either past disappointing events or future worries, and we are therefore not present in our lives, we must ask ourselves: where are we? The consequences of not paying attention in our own lives, or being present, are pretty significant, especially as we get older. Regrets over things that didn't matter that much after all, and explosions or reactions that we allowed to take over our minds and lives, can be averted or at least diluted through some simple mindfulness practices.

So, if mindfulness is about 'just being here now', then how do you get into the present moment? The simple answer? By taking some good, long deep breaths and consciously coming into the here and now. Try holding your breath for more than ten seconds if you don't believe me, and see if you can think of anything else! As we saw in Chapter 2, deep breathing allows our parasympathetic nervous system (PNS) to take over and do its calming job: rest, repose and repair. Our stress response system, our sympathetic nervous system (SNS), is triggered when we feel that the demands or pressures placed on us are more than we think we can cope with. Taking three minutes to breathe deeply and purposefully allows each part of your body to relax, breaks the panic response signal to our brain's amygdalae, and allows the brain and body to calm *themselves*.

Your breath is something that is always with you, and even though you may not have thought about it very much before, your breath can tell you a lot about how you are feeling. Our breath becomes fast when we are anxious, but when we are calm or even asleep, it slows right down. Sometimes, if we are nervous, we can hold our breath without even realising we are doing it. See if you can notice how your own breath is right now, in this moment? If you are holding it, let it go with a gentle exhalation.

Remember, your breath is like your old friend, there since the day you were born. Taking a breath was the first thing each one of us did. Anytime you feel anxious, angry or upset, remember that you can use your breath to help you. It soothes your SNS, and allows your body and mind to calm down. We can practise calm breathing at work, at home and in the water... anywhere, in fact. We just need to remember to do it!

EXERCISE
CALM BREATHING

Read through the steps in this exercise first, as some parts require you to close your eyes. You might want to record them onto your phone's voice recorder and play them back. Or just read, pause – and do.

- Find a comfortable sitting position (this can be indoors on a chair, or outside next to the water).
- Close your eyes: imagine your eyelids are made of heavy concrete and they are so heavy you must close them...
- Take three deep breaths in and out... 'sniffing in' through your nose deeply, and 'blowing out' long, slowly and gently, through your mouth. Do this again, breathing in, and slowly out, and once more, in...
  And as you breathe out, imagine letting go of all your worries from this day, as if they are floating away in a cloud, high into the sky... Inhale, exhale...
- Now, breathing normally, sense the top of your head relax, your hair and scalp soft...

- Feel your face soften, your eyes are closed, your jaw relaxed, breathing in and out.
- Let go of any stiffness in your neck.
- Feel your shoulders drop and relax.
- Breathing in and out, let go of any tension in your chest...
- Feel how your breath makes your stomach rise and fall, breathing in and out...
- Make your stomach soft, breathing slower and deeper there, in and gently out...
- Feel relaxed in your upper back, your mid back and your lower back.
- Let go of any tension in your hips, your legs, your feet and toes.
- Breathe in and out, and let your arms relax; allow your hands and fingers to let go and relax.
- Now take a big breath in through your nose. As you breathe out, allow your *whole body* to feel relaxed and rested, from the top of your head all the way down to your feet... Breathing in, and slowly out... your whole body, relaxed, soft and free from all worry...
- Allow this moment of calm and peace to fill your body. It feels so nice to rest.
- Take three final deep breaths in, and out; in and out, in, and slowly out. Open your eyes when you are ready, and let your gaze adjust to the light in the space you are in.

Notice how that felt for you. Know that by doing this calm breathing, you are giving your mind and body a rest, allowing your neural pathways to come off high alert, and allowing your body to relax and repair itself. Taking a few minutes each day to do this simple exercise will lower your stress levels and help you function better and feel better. (Flick back to Chapter 2 for the science and research on this!)

Our breath is the cornerstone of mindfulness. We all suffer from 'monkey mind' at times, where our inner thoughts jump about like a monkey from the past to the present, back and forth, leading us a merry dance. When we want to bring our monkey mind back from such past ruminations, or future-tense projections, we can focus on our breath and very simply say to ourselves, 'Just be here now.' When I teach young people in my ChillSquad wellbeing sessions, we regularly stop when I ding my wind chime and immediately everyone takes three big breaths in and out as I say, 'Breathing in, I am just here now; breathing out, all is well.' This acts as a lovely reset for any task, any moment, or any difficulty we might be having.

The Seven Principles of Mindfulness

Jon Kabat-Zinn speaks of the seven main principles of mindfulness – and these are useful to think about for ourselves, for others, new situations, and even in relation to bluespace. Let's look at them and how we can adapt them.

1. Non-Judging

This is a hard one! Try to pay attention to your moment-by-moment experiences without getting *caught up in* your own opinions about what you or others are doing, or your likes, dislikes and preferences. Having a constant stream of judgements combined with reactions to them is mentally exhausting (these include thoughts such as 'this is ridiculous', 'my boss is an idiot', 'this is so boring', 'why is this happening, I can't bear it' and so on). Mindfulness asks us to step back from this judging because it locks us into reactions we may not even be aware of, and it can stop us from seeing things as they really are.

A practical way of helping with this is to describe or label something that's going on; for example, instead of getting annoyed with a colleague or family member who is not saying or doing something we want them to, we might pause to take a breath and silently say, 'Person talking... person talking', so that we can make a better response to the situation. We can apply this to our conflicting desire/resistance to getting in the water if the conditions are not 'perfect'. For example, if it is raining, or the sea is colder than we like, we can say to ourselves as we breathe in and out, 'there is rain...', or 'cold water... cold water...' and breathe in, breathe out. (Although, to be fair, swearing at cold water seems to help too!) Responding, rather than *reacting* (usually coupled with an *emotion* such as fear, anger, annoyance) is a key takeaway for mindfulness practice in any space.

Try This

Over the next few days, try to notice how much you judge things both verbally and with your internal dialogue. Watch how keeping a stream of likes and dislikes and critical opinions going is pretty tiring! See if you can switch to descriptions accompanied by breaths. Remember that we cannot control everything, or everyone and their behaviour; we can only control our own response to them. Our breath brings us back to the present moment and to ourselves.

---

2. Patience
The key idea here is to remember that 'things unfold in their own time'. We often become impatient when we want to rush things along if we don't like how they

currently are. Much patience is needed when parenting children, for example, or if working on lengthy projects – but like the life cycle of a butterfly, each stage will come when it is supposed to, and this will be different for each individual or project. Trying to teach a caterpillar to fly is pointless!

Try This

When we are in bluespace, asking the tide to hurry up – to go out or come in faster – gets us nowhere. This is a good metaphor for being patient with things we have no control over in life. We can practise patience with ourselves too if we are new to outdoor swimming – it may take time to get over our nerves, our resistance to the changing temperatures, or to build up our stamina and courage. That's OK. Nature and bluespace teach us to be patient, and that things happen at the pace they are supposed to.

---

3. Beginner Mind

This principle allows us to be open to *new possibilities*, even with the same people, places, job or situation. Often our own preconceptions of what we are sure we 'know' stop us from seeing things how they really are, and therefore we get stuck, frequently in negative interactions or judgements about our present, past or future. Beginner mind says to us that if we choose to see it, each moment, experience, practice and day is new. This is important for adults and children too, to allow them to escape from a 'label' or box – from being 'the sporty one' or 'the shy one', for instance, and to start with a new slate.

Try This

Each swim or encounter next to water is different and allows us to practise beginner mind. The weather, the wind, the conditions, the colours are different... If we had a bumpy swim last time, today's encounter may be different. If we had a bad day yesterday, today is a new one. Our senses respond in different ways depending on these external conditions and, indeed, our own internal state of mind changes on any given day. Immersion in water allows for a cleansing of sorts too. The sea, lake or river can physically wash away our worries and allow us to begin again.

4. Trust

This mindfulness principle is about trusting our own intuition. To do this properly, we must allow ourselves to become quiet, so we can listen without busyness. Taking even five minutes a day to breathe quietly and just be with yourself allows your mind this space. Allow time every month or so to write about yourself in a notebook – where are you at in your life (your work, family, relationships, sense of life purpose)? – and make some plans for what you can do to change anything you aren't happy with. We will go into this in more detail in a later exercise in this chapter. What is your intuition telling you? Trust your own authority, your inner voice; you are not here to compare yourself to other colleagues, parents or family members. Ultimately you must live your own life. Trust in that.

Try This

The water, despite the fear it can induce, asks us to trust it in a way too. A simple exercise in trust is to float. Next time you are in the water (this works just as well in shallow water, if you are nervous of deeper water), mindfully bring your attention to anything that is troubling you, that you cannot seem to solve or control; then take some deep breaths in and out – and allow yourself to float. Trust the water to hold you, and it will... Breathe, relax, and trust that these worries will work out in the best way they can, or how they are supposed to. Allow your reactions to them to soften, and put your trust in the water to hold you up.

5. Non-Striving

This is a really hard principle to apply in a world that has become preoccupied with doing, achieving and success. Workplaces and schools are, by their nature, results and success oriented. We can, however, choose to unpick what achievement and success really *mean* to us. Have a think about that now. What does success mean to you? Does this come from your parents, others or yourself? Is there conflict between what you want for yourself versus what others expect of you? Knowing who we are and what our *own* values really mean to us is an important anchor as we navigate our lives. With mindful meditation, the only goal is to be with yourself, observe, watch, accept... From this point of calm, and with a clear mind, we may then choose options that position us in a direction of fulfilment.

Engagement with water can really encourage non-striving. Rivers and oceans do not compete with each other to be the fastest, the largest or to have the biggest waves or the calmest surface. They just are how they are, and each has its own character. When we immerse ourselves in water, it is worth remembering that we do not have to strive at all. Although there are, of course, lots of outdoor activities that are competitive (such as sailing, rowing, triathlons and lots more), many outdoor swimming groups are there mainly for the watery wellbeing and the company. Hannah spoke of her swimming group to me with love, saying that, 'Not once has anyone ever asked me how far I've swum.' Water allows us to just 'be', if indeed we remember to let it.

6. Acceptance

This is closely related to non-judging in so far as it is about coming to terms with 'what is'. Permitting ourselves, perhaps, to accept that we cannot always force situations or people to be how we would prefer them to be. This doesn't mean giving up accepting that a hurt be unacknowledged, but rather, it is about allowing a peace to come to our *own* selves – and this is often a state of mind that gives us permission to take the right course of action (e.g., 'I accept I am overweight, I observe it and calmly take the action I choose to take at this moment'; or, 'I have been badly hurt by this person/situation, I see my own pain and I allow myself to let this person/situation go now'; or, 'I accept that I am tired and worn out, I acknowledge this and give myself permission to rest'). There is sense of letting go of our reactions to 'I got what I didn't want and I didn't get what I did want' in life or love or work… And then we can find peace with our situation, or seeing it clearly, calmly take the action we need to take.

Try This

The water teaches us acceptance in so many ways; for example, 'I accept that it is cold or raining, and I choose to not react angrily; instead, I get my things and throw myself into the lake, watching the raindrops dance on the surface – I am wet anyway, and life is good!' Or, 'I accept that my body is not perfect, is bigger, smaller or creakier than I would like it to be… but I dress it in swimwear and allow the water to take my weight. I move with ease and gratitude in nature, in water, where I feel at one with myself and this bluespace.' And, 'I accept that this man or woman beside me is a faster or more confident swimmer, and that is OK, I am getting what *I* need from this moment'. And even, 'I accept that my brain is tired, that my emotions are low. I take my breath and as I exhale, I pour these feelings into this living water, which accepts me without judgement. I am part of it, and it is part of me.'

---

7. Letting Go

This final principle of mindfulness encourages us to review what we are holding on to in our lives, such as a particular story or an opinion of someone or something that does not serve us well anymore. Letting go encourages non-attachment (this can be to gratification as well as to pain). It can be hard to let go of the stories in our lives, or to forgive those who have caused us pain. Water encourages us to literally wash away anything we don't need. We feel better after a shower, a swim or a bath.

EXERCISE
RELEASE

Preferably do this exercise when you are in bluespace.

- Just for a moment, close your eyes and think of something you have difficulty in letting go of. Bring that into your mind now, taking several deep breaths. What does it feel like to remember it? Where in your body do you feel it? What are your thoughts and feelings like in this moment?
- Now, imagine this event/relationship/issue being made to dissolve – like salt dissolving ice, a raft floating away on the horizon, or a balloon floating away high into the sky with this issue inside it, up and away, forever.
- Next, tune in to yourself. What does it feel like for this to be gone? How are your body, your feelings and your mind now?
- Imagine if you allowed yourself to really let go of this... What difference might it make to you as a person? Not judging who or what was right or wrong; just letting go?
- Breathe in and out, and just relax for a moment while you consider this choice.
- The next time you get in the water, or visit bluespace, try this exercise again and see if doing it there helps you in any way. If you are by the sea or lake, pick up a pebble and let it represent your difficult issue – then throw it into the sea and let it go. If you are by a river or stream, pick up a leaf or twig, let it represent the challenging issue and throw it into the moving water; allow the issue to be carried away downstream.

Water encourages us to let go – to watch in awe as we witness the power of the waves, the rushing water of a river, the constant ebb and flow of the tides. We have no control over them, they just are. We too can just 'be', if we so choose.

Try This

Next time you stand at the edge of the sea or ocean, as the waves come up the shoreline, breathe in and silently say the word 'peace', and then exhale as the waves drop away again, silently repeating the words 'let go'. Breathing in peace with the incoming waves, breathing out and letting go of everything you don't need in that moment, allowing the backwash to take it away from you. No effort, just let the water and your breath do this for you together…

So, we've looked at a snapshot of mindfulness and some of the principles and practices of 'being'. I think there are many overlaps between these notions of being present – without judgement, aware of our thoughts – and the essence of bluespace. Being in or near water allows us to be free of so much: our self-judgement, our busy minds or physical pain. We can learn a lot from it. When you are next in bluespace, your river, lake, ocean, sea or stream, try to focus just on that present moment: the gift of water, of your place in nature and your breath. Moment by moment, non-judging, awareness and attention.

Doing and Moving

Switching now from stillness to movement, let's think about how we move our bodies in water. This, for many people, is the essence of bluespace wellbeing – just getting stuck in to the bare element of water in all its glory! Many would argue that there is nothing more mindful than getting into water: you are immediately in your body, noticing the temperature and your own responses. We can think of this idea of 'embodiment' and water in different ways.

The simplest way to move in water is to *swim* in it… just you and your body. Depending on the time of year and where you live, you can dress your body in neoprene and other accoutrements, but essentially, it is just about you and your own body moving through the blue. We start, as young children, by paddling in bluespaces. Listen to the shrieks of delight coming from any toddler on the beach as the sea 'gets' them and you will know pure joy!

Many children are taught to swim indoors, in hot, structured and chlorinated swimming pools. How different nature's bluespaces are! When we swim outdoors we must take on the weather and notice how the water itself is moving. We are *connected* to it as we put our bodies into it. How could we not be? When I ask people how swimming helps them feel well, they usually answer in a variety of ways. Katherine says, for her, it is:

> *The routine of my swims – I have regular times, beaches and company. This 'same day, same place, same people' swimming rests my brain. The familiarity feels safe. I miss the salt on my skin. I love seeing it, feeling it and tasting it all day after a swim, reminding me of how good it felt in the water. I particularly love pulling out small pieces of shingle from my hair for the rest of the day and when the wind whips it into my face I can taste the brine. I can feel good for the whole day after a swim aided by these little reminders.*

So bluespace swimming gives us a whole 'sensory hit' at once: the motion, the exercise, the taste… and the feeling lasts well beyond the moment itself for many of us. For others, swimming brings joy, with one person I spoke to noting that:

Unlike any other exercise, which can become more chore-like (to me), wild swimming is pure positivity. It's like a fresh start to life; every single time it brings creative clarity and, it seems, new synaptic connections, solving challenges that have been rattling about in my mind for a while. I wake up in the morning and check Magic Seaweed [the sea-conditions website] before I even look at texts or emails.

For many bluespace swimmers, this 'doing' or 'moving' in water is integral to everyday life, and many are dependent on it for their physical and mental wellbeing.

There are other ways into the water too, however. Some love to dive deep underwater, using oxygen tanks and flippers to emulate sea life itself! There is a quietness and wonder under the sea that offers peace and escape like nothing else. We can also move *with* the water using boards and boats of different varieties. There is a wonderful book by Sam Bleakley called *Mindfulness and Surfing* that looks at not only the history of surfing but how it makes us feel well.[2] I learned to surf when I was in my mid-thirties and it was a revelation! I can attest that surfing is one of the purest forms of mindfulness there is. Lying on your surfboard and watching the waves, reading them, then choosing which one to catch, turning, paddling hard – and then! – that moment when you jump to your feet and feel the wave lift you and your board aloft, as if flying through the water itself. It is momentary ecstasy. And hugely addictive! Of course, it doesn't always come together perfectly – I've nose-dived, been wiped out and buffeted like nobody's business – but while you are surfing your mind is fully occupied with the water and what it's doing. It is very hard to resist the lure of good clean waves on a blue-water day.

Living in Brighton as I now do, good surf rarely appears; that is usually the realm of holidays to Cornwall, Portugal, Lanzarote and Ireland. So, I joined the masses and bought a stand-up paddleboard (SUP) recently. These bring a different experience of movement in the water. Many people use them in rivers and lakes as well as the sea, so they are more of an all-round piece of equipment. There is great peace in sitting, kneeling or standing on a board (once you get past the wobbling). Being out on the water and watching the landscape from that vantage point makes the world look different. When you are out there, you feel very much part of the water. The quiet rhythm and swish of the paddle as it hits the water can be meditative and calming too.

EXERCISE
MINDFUL SEEING (FOR PADDLEBOARDING)

This is a simple mindfulness exercise for anyone who has access to a stand-up paddleboard, or who might want to hire one. (If you don't have access to one, you might like to try out this exercise in a safe, non-tidal bluespace on a lilo or inflatable while you are on holiday.) I have often lain down flat on my own board, hands folded on my stomach, while cloud gazing and doing some deep-breathing. I highly recommend it!

- Climb aboard your SUP and paddle calmly to a spot where you are not close to others or any distractions.
- Now secure your paddle in its hold. Sit cross-legged, if it is comfortable for you to do so. (Alternatively, hang both legs into the water, sitting astride your board.)
- Fold your hands together, palms up, in your lap, and take three deep breaths in and out. Notice your breathing and bring your attention to slowing it down, breathing in and slowly out.
- Now bring your gaze to the water directly beside you. Notice its colour, its texture, its movement, its smell, its transparency. Breathe in and out as you make a note of those descriptive words that come to mind as you look with curiosity at this water.
- Remember not to judge what you are seeing: you are just noticing, describing and breathing.

- Next, bring your gaze to shoreline. Notice what you can see. You may wish to silently repeat words such as 'buildings, trees, sand, people, hills, a jetty, rocks, pebbles', or whatever it is you can see in the bluespace you are in at that moment. Breathe in and out deeply three more times.
- Finally, draw your gaze towards the sky. As you breathe in and out, notice its colour, its light, the shape of any clouds there may be. Are they stationary or moving? Is there anything else you can see in the sky? How do the shoreline, the trees or other objects meet the sky? Can you notice any shapes or patterns as you look calmly and with intention?
- Now, taking a final deep breath in, look down at your own upturned palms, connecting your breath with your body and this water you are on. Notice your surroundings with gratitude, and allow your body to once again return to its moving position as you carry on through the water in a peaceful motion, back to shore.

When we feel anxious or worried, focusing on sensory inputs (sight, smell, sounds) can help us to cut the neural pathways to our amygdalae panic centre in our brains. Combining this with breathwork and the intentional noticing of our surroundings – for instance, the *feel* of the water on our limbs – is a powerful way to come back into our bodies and the space we are in.

This peaceful approach is not for everyone, however. As mentioned at the start of this chapter, many people are drawn to speed and the wind mixed with water. For some there is no greater thrill than windsurfing, kitesurfing, kayaking or sailing. These are not calm, contemplative water sports, but who says wellbeing only comes from quiet? Lots of people feel the need to quite literally blast the wind through their minds, out on the open water – twirling, twisting and turning, working with the energy of the wind and the water together. As we saw in Chapter 2, there is a close relationship between body and mind, between physical and psychological wellbeing. Do what works for you on any given day.

There is, of course, no compulsion to be either in or under the water – we can simply walk *beside* water in a myriad of bluespaces, and this too improves our wellbeing. Weather, time, conditions, equipment, or sometimes the mere faff of getting ourselves organised, mean that we can't always get *into* the water. Going for a walk next to the sea, the lake, the river, canal or pond can calm our minds beautifully. As our bodies age, the need for gentle movement may replace our earlier active selves. It is no accident that many retirement and nursing homes are found by the sea. I've watched pedal bikes being cycled along the Sussex seafront in all weathers, which are adapted with a front seat to hold two elderly people, tucked up warm inside. Smiles, waves and joy for the caregiver, the recipients and all who pass by. If I am lucky enough to live to an old age, this is definitely the way I want to travel!

Community

'Community' is a word we hear a lot. If I were writing this book with only my academic hat on, I'd be tempted here to go into a deep narrative on how the term 'community' can be conceptually constructed across different socio-cultural contexts and the like. But I won't! Community, I think, very simply, is a sense of belonging to something, or to somewhere. It's quite a fluid idea. For lots of communities, you don't have to do much to belong; for example, being Irish abroad makes you part of the 'Irish diaspora community', while living on your street makes you part of the community of that place, or having a certain religious practice makes you part of a faith community perhaps. But the sense of belonging you get from being part of a community depends, I think, on the extent to which you actively engage with it, or it with you. And then, how it makes you *feel*.

I spoke in the last chapter about how 'social wellbeing' is one aspect of what it means to be well. Community, in essence, is what sums this up. Feeling part of something, where you share a common interest – and where there is mutual support, fun, inclusion, kindness and togetherness – is an intangible golden gift in life. As humans we often try to feel like we fit in, or we belong. At a deep psychological level, this gives us a sense of security and an anchor point from which to then go and be ourselves. Many communities run on the premise of conformity. Not so the bluespace wild swimming communities I have come across!

There are many types of walking, sports and swimming communities who use bluespace as their core environment. Most gather because of their love of the water and how it makes them feel. Add in a group of other like-minded humans and we have the recipe for all facets of wellbeing – physical, mental *and* social. It is a beautiful cocktail to behold. When I asked people in my research what it is about being in bluespace that makes them feel well, this notion of community came up time and again. One woman replied that, for her, wild swimming is about the 'peers I swim with – a pod of wonderful women and it's the laughter, smiles on the surface of the water, the serenity, the chats and then the cake!' (Cake appears as a common theme amongst groups of swim communities!) Part of the concept of community is that of sharing, and sharing is abundant in all of these groups. Sharing advice on what to wear in different conditions, where to swim, and, of course, sharing goodies afterwards. One of my pals' 'swim tin' has become infamous – a box of post-swim, energy-boosting delights!

Watery communities are somewhat unique, I think, in that they are not always based on 'one place', nor on one particular type of person. There is a reluctance to stratify or label people according to their work, income, family status or (for most) their physical strength. The common bind is a love of getting in the water. This identity seems particularly strong amongst open water swimmers (some say 'wild swimmers' while others say 'outdoor swimmers'; the phrasing doesn't really matter!) and surfers. There is a sense of sharing the best of the water, so everyone can have a good experience in it. Social media has, of course, allowed for all of this to be more democratic. We can all be part of information-sharing now in an easy, accessible way. Most groups have their own Facebook pages, and/or WhatsApp groups where conversations ping back and forth daily.

Acceptance of each other is another aspect that is implicit in many bluespace communities. I went to a great workshop on 'body positivity' that was held outdoors on the beach in Brighton as part of Mental Health Awareness week in 2019. There was lots of affirmative talk about not judging ourselves, being kind to a body that works and undoing lots of societal conditioning about what our bodies 'should' look like. One of the things that stuck in my head was: 'How do you get a beach body?' Answer: 'Take your body to the beach!' There. Undoing all the superficial sun tanning, bikini and dieting marketing in one fell swoop! Being part of an outdoor swim community gives people confidence, I think, to be themselves. And bluespace, I firmly believe, facilitates that. The sea, the river, the lakes do not care what size or shape your body is. Nature comes in all forms, and so do we.

This sense of belonging to a loosely formed group that loves the water is often referred to as being part of a tribe, a flock, or a squad of some sort. An implicit sense of looking after each other in the group. There are also fewer opportunities to make new friends as you grow older, while doing something new, which is not related to work, schools or children. Especially for women. This sisterhood of outdoor swimming is implicitly valued in so many conversations I've heard.

There is a wonderful book called *I Found my Tribe* by Ruth Fitzmaurice that I really love. [3] It describes how a mother found herself coping with five children while her husband was diagnosed with terminal motor neurone disease. One day at the coast, she connected with another woman whose husband had been badly injured in a motorbike accident. Naming themselves the 'tragic wives club' with a brilliant sense of macabre humour, they found solace in the wild Irish Sea, as it absorbed their grief, anger and frustrations. Their tribe grew from there and has inspired many others to come together to support each other, in the water, beyond 'just swimming'. And I think that's what bluespace gives us – more than just the water itself somehow.

The Salty Seabirds

I mentioned earlier how I joined a wonderful wild swimming community in Brighton called the 'Salty Seabirds'. [4] This social enterprise raises funds through their online wild swim shop (Seabirds Ltd) to help women from all backgrounds to access the water.

It sounds simple, really. Just get in the sea – it's right there, isn't it? Maybe physically, the option to 'just jump in' is possible for many, such as the able-bodied and the psychologically strong. But for some of us – perhaps those working at home by themselves, or tackling mental health issues, depression, poor self-esteem, shyness, or a whole range of other possible situations – getting in the sea either alone or with others can seem like a very daunting thought. Without the support of a community, it is almost impossible for a lot of people who are vulnerable in all sorts of ways to even begin to wild swim.

I attended an early workshop at the inception of Seabirds – where we were gently asked to talk about our own barriers to getting in the water. Fears of deep water, of not being a 'proper swimmer', of going in the water alone, what to wear, where to get into the water, embarrassment over our bodies, and a limited understanding of tides and currents, and much more, were all commonly expressed worries. People shared stories of depression and anxiety, and hopes that the water would help. It was soul-baring stuff for a small group of strangers. And when we finished talking, we all tentatively got into the sea.

I remember the day clearly: it was absolutely lashing with rain and a howling south-westerly wind sweeping up the soaked promenade in Brighton. And yet there was laughter and screaming as we waded into the sea. If we could do this soul-exposure in these conditions, there was hope surely? That day marked a turning point for me. A moment where I had swum alone, or walked by the sea to heal and rebalance myself, shifted – to one where I found others who did the same. And talked about it openly. Life would never be the same, in the best way possible.

From that workshop emerged a self-servicing Facebook page where membership of Brighton's Salty Seabirds grew from an initial dozen of us or so up to almost 2,000 people. We post times and suggestions for where we are free to swim, and whoever fancies it just comes along. Sometimes there are three or four of us, sometimes up to forty. The colder the better! This salty community also provides a reason and focus to get in – it offers company for mothers at home or solo workers, and human contact and contact with the water itself.

The simplicity of the group's format – suggest, swim and connect – at whatever depth (literal and metaphorical) has been its success. We are a motley crew of bobbers, crawlers, dippers and splashers. There are flasks of tea and

Tupperware boxes of home-baking. Chat if needed, or smiles and waves if not. As one member observed, 'It's the giggles and the banter, and the conversations on the beach. I miss the feeling of being held physically or metaphorically by the sea, and the flock.'

I'm into my third year of it now, and without intending to, have become an all-year-round swimmer. No wetsuit (everyone always asks that next). The sharp jolt of cold water brings you immediately into your body and temporarily suspends all other worries. The lovely Seabird flock provides all the things a bluespace community should: a love of the sea, tolerance and acceptance of each other's physical and mental conditions, kindness, mutual support, deep chats if needed, flippant humour, and lots of cake. What could be better?

If you are reading this and wondering, 'Should I try to find the courage to join an outdoor swimming group?' my advice is yes, just do it! Look up the group and join on Facebook first. Get a feel for the tone of the comments. Some groups may be more focused on swim 'training' – fitness, distance swimming and so on. Others will be a mix of social and the physical aspects; others, like Salty Seabirds, will meet mainly for the joy of it. Find your tribe, or, if there isn't the kind of bluespace community you feel suits you where you live, go out and *start one up*! You won't regret it.

For anyone new to outdoor swimming, the temperature can be off-putting at first. That combined with shyness or not knowing anyone can seem like huge barriers when you are first thinking of getting out more into bluespace. I've talked about the lovely aspects of finding your tribe in a swim community, but you might also want to practise overcoming the 'gasp reflex' that is normal when you first get used to outdoor swimming.

EXERCISE
BREATHING ON ENTERING COLD WATER

With practice, you can adapt the general breathing exercise to focus your breath, very specifically, as you get into the sea, ocean, lake or river.

- As you step into the water, notice if you are holding your breath. If you are, allow yourself to let it go, to exhale gently.
- As you go deeper into the water, perhaps to waist depth, again notice your breath – allow it to regulate... Inhale deeply, exhale slowly, inhale and blow out quite forcefully and for as long as you can manage, in through your nose and out through your mouth...
- As you come to chest depth, again take several deep breaths in and out. The number of repetitions will depend on how well adapted to cold water you are, so take your time.
- Direct your gaze to the horizon and the sky. Begin to tread water, if you are comfortable doing so, and focus on your breath, inhaling and exhaling more regularly now, until your breath becomes even. If you like, you can count to keep your focus. (If you are not confident treading water, you can keep your feet touching the bottom.)
- Imagine a rectangle with two short ends on the left and right, and two long ends on the top and bottom. Move your breath around the rectangle as you breathe in and out.
- So, beginning bottom left, inhale for the count of two as you go up the short side of your rectangle and exhale for the count of four as you go across the top of your rectangle. Then breathe in for two seconds as you move down the far, short side of the rectangle,

and finish with an exhalation for the count of four at the bottom, long end of the rectangle.

- You can go around your rectangle once, or for as many breaths as you want to. If you like, you can float on your back and try a few rectangle breaths.
- For some people, this practice helps to regulate the cold temperature; for others, it helps them to cope with a fear of the waves or the deep (remember, our breath cuts the panic signal to our anygdalae); and for others still, it helps them simply to come into the present moment and let go of the rest of their day.
- Again, when you finish your breathing, notice how it feels, and see if you can compare your own before and after state.

Water and breath combined form a complete and utter force of calm, strength and presence!

Gratitude

Appreciating what we do have, rather than focusing on what we don't have, is an important part of feeling strong inside. Gratitude, as one of my lovely kids in ChillSquad once said, is all about having a 'great attitude'. Why should we practise gratitude? Well, it allows us to shift our thinking, even for a moment, to a calmer and more content perspective... Or, to put it more simply, when we remember things to be thankful for, we *feel better*, and things don't seem so bad after all.

If we practise being grateful regularly (at night, for example, think of three things you are grateful for that day) this literally 'trains our brains', creating positive neural pathways and gradually shifting us to a more optimistic outlook. Practising gratitude (by this I mean either making a list, saying out loud, or *thinking* of what we are grateful for, regularly) releases a powerful chemical called 'dopamine' to the prefrontal-cortex part of our brain, which makes us feel good.

Research shows that repeating certain thoughts over and over again in our minds makes certain neural pathways stronger. Think about drawing a line on a piece of paper: if you go over and over that line many times, the pattern gets more defined; the impression on the paper is deeper and stronger. For some of us, there is a tendency to default to the negative in our minds, perhaps without even noticing it. We all know people whom we almost have to brace ourselves to see, expecting that there will be complaints, negativity and a tendency to think the worst of everything, right? Their negative neural pathways have become stronger because of the *habit* of thinking negative thoughts. The good news is we can change this pattern and switch our neural pathways to more positive ones. How? Very simply, *through the daily practice of gratitude.* And this, wonderfully, is a choice.

Remembering to be thankful for small things, every day, releases dopamine in our brains and strengthens positive neural pathways in our brain. Having negative, worried or angry thoughts over and over again creates a superhighway to our brain's stress/panic centre, the amygdalae. It's a matter of practice and noticing ourselves when we do it. I encourage children in my ChillSquad sessions to imagine they have a switch on the back of their heads. When they notice themselves or others getting into negative, critical thoughts or words, they – or someone in their class, home, or family – can flick the switch to the positive and grateful side. Done with humour, this really works! 'Flick your switch!' is a common call in our home. Try it.

So, how do we connect gratitude and bluespace? I think, for most humans, looking at an expanse of water naturally makes us feel grateful. I say out loud at least once a week, 'I am so lucky to live here by the sea.' And I make sure my children are grateful for the childhoods they have in this bluespace too. But we can practise this form of gratitude on trips to water, days out, holidays or even stolen moments here and there. The key is to remember to do it.

EXERCISE
EVERYDAY GRATITUDE

The thinking, writing and reading of pieces of gratitude release dopamine in our brains and strengthen our neural pathways. So why not create your own gratitude bank?

- Find a large jar, a shoebox or other vessel, and make a colourful label for it with the word 'Gratitude' written on it.
- Each day, you (and others in your home if you share a space) get a scrap of paper and write down one thing you are grateful for that day. Then fold it up and put it in your jar or box.
- Then maybe two or three times a year – at Christmas, New Year's Eve, a birthday, anniversary, or another significant date for you – open the jar or box and take turns to read (or read to yourself) all the things you have been grateful for in that period.

Try This

If creating a gratitude bank feels like hard work, then a simple alternative is every day at bedtime, before you switch off the light, say out loud, write or call to mind three things you are grateful for that day. If you are having a bad day and nothing seems to be going well, you can still be grateful for hands that work, legs that move, fresh air to breathe, and so on. Thinking of these small, taken-for-granted things shifts our thoughts and improves our wellbeing.

We are never too old or young to practise gratitude. Even my little six-year-old nephew, Francis, calls out his father when he is being grumpy and says, 'Dad, I think you need to go and do your gratefuls!' Gratitude works – it is one of the simplest but most often overlooked ways back into our own balance and wellbeing.

EXERCISE
PEBBLE GRATITUDE

Water is the perfect place to remind us of the simplicity and power of gratitude. I have watched people in tears as they've done the following pebble exercise in bluespace, and told each other how they are grateful for each other.

- Sit by the sea or lake, and bring a pebble or stone with you or look around and find one. It doesn't have to be perfect.
- Looking out at the water in front of you, take three deep breaths in and out, saying silently to yourself, 'Thank you, water, for being here.'
- Then, close your eyes and touch the stone in your hands. Notice its shape and texture. Bring your attention to how it feels. Is it sharp or smooth? Does it feel cold or warm? Breathe and notice what you can about this pebble with your eyes closed.
- Now, open your eyes and look closely at the pebble in your palm. What can you see when you really look hard? In your mind, as you breathe in and out, name the colours, any cracks or imperfections. Does what you see match with what you felt a moment ago, with your eyes closed?
- Does it matter if the pebble is not perfect? Do you like it any less? If not, then allow this message to remind you that you do not have to be perfect either to be of value.
- As you hold the pebble, look at the water, or close your eyes, if you prefer, and think of ten things you are

grateful for, that money cannot buy. You might want to begin by silently repeating: 'I am grateful for this space, I am grateful for this sea/this lake/this river, I am grateful for the earth, I am grateful for nature' – then add your own...

- A powerful additional step is to *share* this exercise with others – for instance with a swimming group or your family – especially if you are going through tough times for any reason.

When we are in bluespace, we can try to remember to trigger gratitude. That way, we can connect one with the other in easier and positive ways both while we are near water and elsewhere in our lives.

Creating

Everyone finds their own way into wellbeing, and for some it is not always about getting into water. There is great peace and reward to be found in being creative. Making art, sculpture or crafting, using the elements of water and the earth itself, is grounding and calming. I have a cousin who is a gifted and well-known sculptor, Noel Scullion. He works with huge chunks of limestone filled with fossils and laid down over millions of years in seabeds. His work often portrays the earth's movement or nature moving with and through the earth.

To see an artist's talent can humble us and give us perspective. Seaside holiday places are often littered with art shops full of images that depict the beauty of water; think of paintings of St Ives, the Florida Keys and the Great Barrier Reef, or photographs capturing tropical island scenes and sunsets – pieces of art that we breathe in and want to take home with us. Making and creating triggers our brain into mindful concentration of the task at hand, and helps to quieten our minds.

Rachel's Story

Nature, and bluespaces in particular, have always inspired me and been my happy place. As my swim story has unfolded, the sights, colours, textures and feelings have appeared more and more in my art. Whenever I'm in nature, whether a green- or bluespace, my eyes are roving over the vistas and horizon. I also notice the details – a shell, an unfurling leaf, or seaweed floating in the swell. My camera roll is full of images that complement those captured by my mind.

A swim, for me, is so much more than just immersion in water, relaxation and time with friends (though it is also all these things). I can't switch off my artist's eye, but it means I experience moments of flow and mindfulness so much more, as my brain is thinking about what I see in front of me. I love the curves of light and shadow on a calm sea, especially nearing sunset. I have chased floating seaweed to photograph it spreading out across the surface! I will never tire of the split vista of water against land and sky, whatever the weather or colour.

I'm now finally developing techniques and mediums to be able to capture these bluespaces in my art. I papercut the shapes of the swell, the silhouettes of my swim friends against the sky or their legs under the water. I'm still working out how to best represent the waves, which were a big part of our winter swims this year! I've started learning watercolour to represent the land and seascapes, in particular the magnificent chalk cliffs where I swim, seen at a swimmer's level. Most of my evenings are taken up with making abstract multimedia pieces inspired by seaweed! I love the way acrylic ink can fade, swirl and pool the same way water does.

Sometimes words feature, often the same phrases used by swimmers to sum up the way we feel about our swims: 'vitamin sea', salty solidarity, blue therapy, swim for the soul. I have also started a series of collages inspired by swimming under the full moon. Nature, blue and green, will always inspire me. The more I swim, the more ideas I have that fill my head and notebooks.

Making our own art, even if we are not artists per se, is a wonderful and mindful thing to do on any shoreline. When I run my WildBlue School sessions with children, we learn about the nature of the coast and water, and then we try to create things with what is there. The children's imaginations floor me every single time. They gather stones, pebbles, shells, seaweed and more with focused glee. They work together to come up with ideas – and then make and create some of the loveliest artworks of nature ever. I've seen seaweed-haired mermaids with layered shell tails, whales drawn in the sand and filled with plastic litter-waste to decry our human negligence, sea-monsters made of driftwood with pebbled eyes and fierce faces, and snapping crabs partially drawn but supplemented with real remnants of crab claws and carapaces. I love seeing every single one. And I especially love hearing their proud and excited explanations of each piece they've found, the story of their ideas and thoughts behind their creations.

Time for some childlike, mindful, creative play?

EXERCISE
BEACHCOMBING SHORELINE
SCULPTURE CREATION

For this exercise, you can work alone as a peaceful meditative practice, or in small groups of two or three (if you are with a swim tribe, for example, or out for the day with family or friends).

- Bring a bucket or small recyclable bag with you to collect things in.
- Arriving at the shoreline, look around and, if you are part of a group, decide how you will divide up the space between you to beachcomb. If you are alone, just begin where you please.

- Look closely at the ground and shoreline beneath your feet, and collect as many different types of items as you can in your bucket or bag.
- These can include pebbles, stones, shells, seaweed, parts of crabs that have been washed up, cuttlebones, mermaid's purses, driftwood, sea-glass – or, if you are in a freshwater place, leaves, weeds, twigs, stones, grasses or whatever your eyes are drawn to.
- Next, find a smooth, flat or undisturbed space to lay out your 'treasure' – and think about how you can arrange what you've found.
- There are many options here – you might want to take a museum-curator approach and draw squares or circles in the sand or soil and place all of the same category of item together, the shells, the stones, etc. or classify them by colour or texture. Or you can make something creative from your own imagination, such as a shape that relates to the space you are in, like a shark or mermaid creation, a castle, an underwater scene, a mandala, a rainbow, a person, or a flower... it's up to you. The joy is in letting your imagination go where it wants to. If you are in a group, discuss some ideas, shortlist and vote!
- When you've finished, sit next to your creation and, if it's peaceful to do so, take three deep breaths in and out – and really notice the colours, textures and shapes of each item in your creation. Notice the colour and movement of the water around you and the sky too... What can you see?
- Breathing in and out, think of curiosity and gratitude. Consider the origin of each item, the wonder of it, and how it got to be here in your possession today. The pebble laid down millions of years ago; the piece of chalk formed of tiny sea-creature skeletons; the mermaid's purse made of one of the strongest substances in

the world and holding its shark eggs safely until they are released into the ocean when they are ready; the driftwood from a faraway groyne; the wildflower whose seeds were spread by the wind, or by a bird soaring in the sky... The flow of a moving river; the peace of a still pond; a freshwater lake that we can swim in, which provides life for so many beings, gouged perhaps by a huge force of glacial ice. Nature is incredible.

- Look at your creation and think of how we are all connected, to each other, the earth and to water. Breathe in creativity; breathe out wonder.
- Before you return from your excursion, take a photo of your creation for your memories. Then please leave everything behind that is natural. These pebbles, seaweed and shells belong in their natural habitat – much as we love to look at them in our homes.

Taking What You Need

What water can do for our wellbeing is a fluid and ever-changing thing. There are moments, days, times, when we need it to be calm and healing; and others when we need to move with it, fast or ferocious, to match a volatile mood or feeling. Water changes, as do we. The principles of mindfulness we've looked at here can enable us to frame our daily lives in a more peaceful way. Remembering to breathe and noticing when we are judging ourselves, others or certain situations, helps to free our minds in a more positive way.

But life will still throw obstacles in our paths and we may often struggle to cope. Grief, fear, anxiety and depression are part of many people's everyday worlds, as we will discuss in the next chapter. There are many different offerings out there to help us deal with all of these. However, bluespace and nature are our constants. Some days you may feel like solitude by the water to ease your mind. Other days, a community, or tribe of folk who love bluespace too, can be the buoy you need to cling to. Whatever your emotions, take time by the water and let it give you what you need.

4

BLUESPACE IN TIMES OF NEED

The previous chapter showed us some of the principles and practices of bluespace wellbeing; how we can be still or move, or create or connect as needed to improve how we feel. But there are times in life when tough situations and experiences will still come our way. Sometimes they are sudden; sometimes they are long wars, with many battles interspersed with peacetime and respite. We can all chart the rollercoaster of our life experiences over time.

Bluespace can be a real place of refuge in difficult times. Occasionally, we may experience fear in water too. Like all challenging situations in life, there are lessons to be learned when we experience fear, pain and loss. Nobody would be likely to choose these feelings as optional character-building experiences, but they come our way, nonetheless.

Overcoming Fear

It feels like an odd thing – to write about the fear of water in a book about bluespace wellbeing. But it's there. You can love something whilst holding a fear or respect for it, I think? When I mentioned the Salty Seabirds in Chapter 2, I described a pilot workshop in which people talked about what they were afraid of when it comes to getting into the water. Understanding our barriers and the challenges we face can go a long way towards helping us to embrace the positive aspects. As a principle of bluespace wellbeing, letting go is important, as are trust, non-judging and patience. We can let go of 'old stories' about ourselves and water that don't serve us well anymore; we can begin to trust ourselves and the water itself – and be patient with ourselves if it takes us time to overcome our fears. And most of all, not judge ourselves for how we interact with water in different conditions, or for our bodies and how they look or what they can do, compared to others.

Focusing on our breath, moment by moment, as we embrace a fear of water is the first small step. Community support and safety-checks are other ways that will help us face our fears. Swim with friends, in safe conditions, at low tide, near lifeguards if they are there, when you are rested, fed and watered. And know your limits – all the good, sound advice you will find in almost any outdoor swimming community.

But our perceptions of water are personal and rooted in our own experiences. For every ten people who love the sea, there is one who is terrified of it. I was reminded of this recently when I had a group of children with me for a WildBlue School session. Integrating some English literacy skills into their learning (see – outdoor classrooms work for *every* subject!), I asked them to use some adjectives to describe the sea. There were shouts of 'exciting', 'sparkling', 'fun', 'blue-green' and 'amazing'. But then came a small hand, shyly raised, whose owner whispered, 'Scary.' I asked the little girl later, away from the group, why she thought the sea was scary. She wasn't sure; it wasn't a place she came to often with her family, she couldn't swim and she just simply didn't like the look of it. It was a good reminder to me not to make assumptions based on my own preferences. In fact, my own twin brother, Richard, only half-jokingly calls the sea 'a lonely life-swallower'. How we shared the same womb-space and have such polar opposite thoughts on water, I can't figure out!

However, there was an occasion some years ago when I had a near-miss with water, as many of you may have had too. It stays with you, doesn't it?

Three years after my mother's death, when I had settled into my new post in the west of Ireland, I asked my boss if he would allow me to go on a career break. It was a risky request as I had only been in the post a relatively short time. But I felt spent. I had held myself together to cope with the aftermath of our tragedy, my family had stopped reeling to some extent, and now I needed to go, to escape and be far away from it all for a while.

This is a common personal theme for me, I've realised – the need to travel, or go, when things are too much, or when I've come out the other side of something difficult. A going, to come back to myself. I felt I had always been the dutiful eldest daughter, the reliable one with the good exam results, who worked hard to get a degree in Trinity and then her PhD – and now it was time to let myself off the hook and be carefree, without context. I booked an around-the-world ticket and took off with my backpack for 14 months.

Water played a big role in my exploration of Central America, the US, Fiji, New Zealand, Australia and Africa. Highlights were fringing-reef snorkelling on the edges of small Fijian islands, diving the Great Barrier Reef, river canyoning in New Zealand and sea kayaking in Queensland. But I almost didn't make it back from one of my bucket-list activities.

I had always wanted to white water raft down the Zambezi River in Africa. It sounded so adventurous and glamorous! Maybe I was on some kind of life-affirming dance with death in all these travels, given what I was running from or trying to make sense of; I don't know. I paid my $100 and excitedly took my spot on the back of the raft, with six other backpackers I didn't know, on the Zambian side of the river, near to Victoria Falls.

It turns out that white water rafting on a grade 5 river is not in fact a happy, clappy, splashy, jolly jape after all. The raft was continuously hurled ferociously sideways, high up into the air, then down again with huge, jarring force. You had only recovered from one forceful rapid when another was upon you.

I wasn't quite sure how it happened – my memory has blocked much of it out – but one minute I was sitting at the back of the raft, and the next I was underneath it in darkness, fighting for my life. In the raft, I had been perched at the back on a hard, wooden 'body-board' (I later found out these were used for airlifting spinal injuries out of the gorge), and as the raft flipped over in a raging torrent of water, the board hit the back of my head and concussed me.

I came to, dazed and in darkness, underneath the large, heavy raft. The raft shot through a three-phase rapid, undulating and crashing up and down on me heavily as I gripped it in terror. Imagine the loud sound of roaring water, the velocity of it, the darkness and the sensation of someone tugging you underwater, all simultaneously.

My life vest meant I wasn't able to swim out and under the raft. In fact, my concussion meant the only thought in my mind was to hold on to the raft for dear life. Within seconds, I was swallowing huge volumes of water, as I inadvertently pulled the small, moving air cavity down on myself, just by holding on.

My energy was quickly and exhaustingly sapped by the force of the river itself. It seemed like hours passed. I didn't know where I was, injured and alone in this dark, roaring, moving space; all I knew was that I now had nothing left in me. They say drowning is peaceful. I think it is, but it also feels like quiet resignation. There was nothing I could do here, nothing. My final thought before I lost consciousness was, 'You paid a hundred dollars to kill yourself, you bloody eejit.'

I came round being given mouth-to-mouth and CPR inside the raft. I have no recollection of how I went from underwater, drowning, to back in the raft. Fellow travellers told me that kayakers had finally caught up with the raft and flipped it back over, to find me unconscious underneath. I was glad to be alive.

The downside was I had a further eight rapids to do before I could get out. The gorge was only as wide as the river itself, so my request to walk the rest of it just wasn't feasible. When we reached the end, I scrambled up the side of the towering canyon, shaking, like an adrenaline-fuelled billy goat. My pulse raced for days and I couldn't shut my eyes to sleep without reliving it all.

Travelling alone and almost dying had shaken my own sense of immortality. I queued up in the village payphone, standing in line, in the dirt, clutching a handful of coins, and managed to ring my sister in New York for about two minutes, to tearfully announce I had almost died. To those around me, it was just another backpacker tale. That moment, however, taught me that water can be treacherous – and that I am mortal. My mother's sudden death had shown me that life can be taken without warning, and now the river had reminded me of that too. Nature's lessons.

Despite the near-death experience in Africa, I learned to surf a few years later on the wild beaches of Cornwall. I loved it beyond any other 'sport' I had ever done. My thirty-something-year-old body wasn't sure what hit it – but my mind felt both the thrill and peace of the waves. It became, and still is, a go-to holiday activity. Flying through the ocean on a piece of moving fibreglass gives you the chance to blissfully forget all else. Childlike, gleeful and completely in the moment. A joy like no other. If you have had a traumatic experience with water, I can really recommend trying to find your way back into it – gently, through doing something that brings you joy. A surf or paddleboard may be the way?

My own fear of water is still with me since that Zambezi episode, however: my legs usually tremble before I go surfing and for the first 15 minutes in the water. I can easily panic if I feel very far from shore while swimming, or if I feel a rip current pull me out. Many of us feel fear when we are out of our depth or when we swim against a changing tide. If I am told to put my face in the water, an irrational terror comes over me. I know this is true for many people I've spoken to. All we need to do is swim within our own comfort zone.

My sea swimming community (and many others, I'm sure) gets a bit overexcited when the 'buoys' appear in the sea for the summer season – separating the swim zone from the boat lanes. There is much chatter of 'swimming out to the buoys', doing laps of them even, or, God forbid, swimming *around* the piers (which jut far out to sea in Brighton)! This talk makes me wobble, a lot. I did swim out to the buoys once at low tide – and I can't say I enjoyed it. I didn't have a moment of, 'See, Catherine, you can do it!' Well, maybe a little. But I know enough about how the sea works to know that no two swims are the same, and maybe next time I might not be as lucky with the conditions! Non-judging, non-striving, trust, beginner mind, patience, just being here now... see? Mindfulness principles are *everywhere* in bluespace!

A little while back, I thought I'd try my first outdoor swimming-pool lesson, to get some kind of 'proper technique' going. Nope, it didn't work. Even though I could stand up in the pool, about halfway into the lesson, I felt a familiar surge of irrational emotion, fears and tears rising. I felt like I was choking. Annoyed with myself, I discussed it with a friend afterwards. She reminded me that deep-seated trauma gets stored in our memory, and our brain's amygdalae – our flight, fight or freeze response sites to stress – are triggered when we recall such trauma. Sometimes this can even be a subconscious response.

So even though I was not in danger in the pool, when I was asked to put my face down (and it wasn't my own choice to do so), the memory and panic were triggered. I questioned then why I needed to swim 'properly' and realised that, actually, I didn't. For me, swimming outdoors is all about looking up at the sky, seeing the colour of the water, and breathing in the horizon. Ploughing along facedown holds little appeal. And with that, I let myself off the hook. My fear of water remains strong, but my love of it way surpasses that fear, and I think that is common for so many of us.

Anxiety and Depression

Many people I've talked to confirm that getting into water, into bluespace, helps to improve their mood or calm their anxiety. Chapter 2 discussed some of the research into water and psychological wellbeing, but here I want to share a few personal insights into some of the felt-experiences of anxiety and depression in relation to bluespace. There won't be any exercises or practical suggestions here, because for many people, these can be serious or chronic conditions that need a range of medical and (for some of us) natural approaches. All I can say – as you may guess – is that getting in the water makes you feel better.

When people are in the throes of a depressive bout, or an episode of anxiety, getting them to the water in the first place may not always be possible. The last thing a person with a severe bout of depression can face is getting out of bed and gathering up swim gear, towels and the like. But we have seen how strengthening our neural pathways – so that our brains make associations between things – is helpful in improving our wellbeing. So, even when we feel low, if we create and practise *the habit* of getting in the water, a neural pattern of positive feedback is there for our brain to default to, even if our conscious mind resists:

water = feel better

This is where a bluespace community comes into its own. Feelings of isolation, sluggishness and the inability to do what serves us best are all symptoms of depression. These are usually accompanied by feelings of shame, denial or guilt. Anxiety makes us overthink and question everything we do – 'How can I do this?', 'I look terrible in a wetsuit', 'What if nobody talks to me?', 'What if *I* don't want to speak to anyone?', 'What if the current gets me?', and so on – like a running tickertape of crushing self-assault. For some, it can be very hard, impossible, often, to verbalise the feelings that accompany depression. Many men, for example find that their world is very performance-driven, and when they are not 'achieving' (often in terms of work expectations), their self-esteem can nosedive. 'We aren't allowed to talk about feeling like a failure,' says Joe. He continues:

We all act like we are fine even if we aren't. When I get depressed, I often feel like I just have to stay inside and not come out until it's over. I usually pretend I'm sick. Sometimes this takes days, sometimes weeks. I feel like I can't move.

One time, about two years ago, when I had a very bad patch and thought I couldn't go on another day, a friend got me down to sea and made me get in with him. It was the last thing in the world I felt like doing. I only did it to shut him up. But then, when I was in there, even for the five minutes it took, I got out of my own head and it helped. Then it helped again the next time. And now I just need it, depend on it. The dark days still come, and I don't know how to talk about them much still, but I do know what to do. Some of us go a few times a week now at 6am, and it gets me through.

Bluespace can help us all, men and women alike, when we are feeling low. For men, there is the opportunity to not strive – to not be the fastest, swim the furthest, or talk about the best gear, goggles or wetsuit, in this peaceful space. Of course, the physical fitness and endorphins that come with vigorous exercise help our wellbeing too. Whatever works for you, do it. Just get in the water!

However, like Joe, we may want to hide ourselves away

until depression or anxiety passes. 'I really should go and get in the sea,' Jane told me, 'but I just can't.' She continued:

I can't move when I feel like this. I feel very alone, inside my head. I have never been able to shift this weight on my own before. Until I found my wild swimming group. Now, if I feel the black dog chasing me, I feel safe enough with a few people in my tribe, who are fellow sufferers, to be honest about it. I can say to them that I'm feeling low, and someone will make a swim arrangement with me for a specific time that day. Some will even come and drive me there. Other times it will be an unspoken bear hug, where I'm not able to verbalise anything... I just need to hit the cold water, hard. It just helps me get through things, in a better way than I would otherwise; I need this tribe, this water.

These experiences are very personal so it's impossible to make generalisations. There is huge vulnerability in admitting to suffering from anxiety or depression. It exposes our soul but also opens a bridge for trust and empathy. The quiet voice inside us that says 'you're not good enough' is held, and repaired, by the water and by others who get into it with us. Almost imperceptibly.

Kath's Story

I have suffered with anxiety and depression for as long as I can remember. I wasn't always aware of what they were, but with hindsight I can see they have always been there. Day-to-day functioning is, for me, the hardest part of my mental illness. I can do it, but I need to factor in rest, relaxation and respite. Where anxiety tells me I can't do something, depression physically stops me from doing it. The thought of doing something, anything, is met with lethargy and avoidance. On the outside, it looks like you can't be bothered, but in reality, you don't know where to start and feel totally overwhelmed. Total exhaustion and tiredness of the wrong kind. At my worst, I have left jobs and relationships; at my best, I am on permanent medication.

The rest and respite I need to counter how overwhelmed I can feel are easily achieved at the beach. You cannot take your phone into the sea. You cannot hear it beeping on the beach when you are in the water. The constant scrolling images and high-pitched sounds are replaced by a never-changing horizon. I swim year round, in freezing temperatures and challenging sea states. By putting myself in these situations on a regular basis, I am exposing my body and mind to stress. Getting into wavy, cold water is stressful for your body and mind, but I cope. My body has adapted to deal with this stress, and it then helps me go on to deal with everyday stress. When I am swimming in these conditions, I can only be concerned about myself, in that moment, in that situation – there is no room to be concerned with anything else.

The sense of achievement of when I 'can' get in the sea, and when I 'do' – in the context of my anxiety and depression – is an incredible feeling. Just leaving the house to go to the beach can seem an insurmountable 'do' on days when I am running on empty. Most of the time I see the world in black and white, devoid of colour, devoid of joy. I can be happy and content, but unadulterated joy is very rare and only happens when I am completely present and in the moment. And these moments are always when I am in the sea. Sea swimming, as a pastime, is joyful. The post-swim high (from cold water) can last for hours after the event. Knowing that the sea is a constant and that I therefore always have a constant supply of joy, just buoys me. And the post-swim, fresh sea air, childlike tiredness is guaranteed to give me a good night's sleep, building up my reserves of resilience to face the next day. Tiredness and exhaustion of the right kind.

Other people think you are mad for swimming in the sea all year round – and I own that label! Being in the sea reminds me that my depression and anxiety are transient, with ebbs and flows like the tide. It provides me with the opportunity to check in with myself, to see if another episode is on the horizon. Although dark *times are part of the disease, sea swimming can provide a break in the clouds. I did not choose to feel this way, but I have chosen how I deal with it on a day-to-day basis.*

I think there is much to be said for the water allowing us moments of pause, to check in with how we are. You are, as Kath describes, completely in your body, and present – the simplest form of mindfulness – when you are in the water. You are negotiating water, temperature, movement, conditions and processing the bluespace landscape around you. It is a different kind of being, one that can help to quell our anxious minds or bodies that do not feel very alive when weighed down with the concrete of depression.

Sometimes, certain stages in our life cycle bring about their own challenges. Many women I know are going through the perimenopause or menopause itself. This is something that can last for years. It certainly has in my own case. As our hormones rage and quell, rise and fall – much like the ocean itself – many of us feel at sea, lost and unsure of ourselves. Many women report low mood, hormone migraines, weight gain and acute attacks of anxiety for the first times in their lives. Some reports are coming out about the benefits of cold water swimming for these menopause symptoms.[6] But like the depression research noted in Chapter 2, more needs to be done so we can say with certainty how and why bluespaces can help with these symptoms. For many (peri-) menopausal women, a wild swimming community offers many of the elements of wellbeing we are examining here: physical wellbeing, cold water that stimulates the vagus nerve, exercise, breath control, presence, community, trust, being *and* doing, moving, overcoming fear, non-judging, and personal growth. Some will value certain elements of this cocktail more than others. For me, it is a wonderful, holistic buffet-table of support – one that is unique to bluespaces and their people.

Grief and Healing

There is something about water that takes your pain away. Throwing your body into cold or crashing waves can allow nature to deflect or absorb what you are feeling. The rage, the sorrow, the aching numbness. And the throes of grief can very much feel like a gasping. A struggle for breath, to keep going in life, when that life of yours has been shattered, never the same again from that moment onwards.

My own mother's death felt like that. An unexpected blow to the head. Sudden, young death brings its own impacts to those going through it. Others experience the long, drawn-out pain of watching a loved one slowly die of a physical disease or of dementia. In both cases, there is a long and slow process of loss. Families pull together, or they don't, and through it all, the rest of the world marches on, cruelly going about its business, despite your pain and struggle. The water is a constant – always there, for when we are ready to go to it. My own grief has been healed hugely by the wild Atlantic coast of Ireland, of countless trips to big surf all over the world, and my beloved everyday water in Brighton. But everyone has their own story to tell.

Josie, an indoor and outdoor swimmer, suffered a huge loss when her fiancé died before their wedding at the age of only 39. She had been training for a 20km sea-trek challenge just before they met. Shared plans and dreams were suddenly shattered, and she felt that in her grief she lost herself and her joy. It took two years before she could face getting in the water again, despite several tearful attempts. Her memories of her fiancé watching her train and their shared holidays by the sea were too much to bear for a long time: 'Our best holiday memories were always of the sea,' Josie says. She continues:

When I moved to Brighton, I found the Salty Seabirds and the healing power of friendships. The sea brought me back to life.

Guilt turned to gratitude and missing him became connecting to him through the crashing waves and the effort it takes, like with grief, to swim through it. Getting back into the water gave me a new challenge. Something positive to focus on and, despite the wind and the jellyfish, the English Channel has been the very best therapy.

Liz cared for her mother, who had terminal cancer, at home. 'I was,' she admits, 'wound up, tight as a drum.' She explains:

So, I started swimming. I knew that I needed a crazy good excuse to get me out of the house, and the challenge of swimming outdoors through the winter months provided that excuse. My best friend introduced me to it during a weekend away by the sea, so I took to the water every week through October, November, December, January, dipping in the marine lake at Clevedon. The temperature of the water got down below 5°C, and I only ever stayed in for a few minutes, but every time I got out of the water I was topped up with a burning tingling fire, brought on by cold water immersion. I felt my body working hard to save me. I felt like it meant I could trust my body to keep me alive, even in the toughest times.

Liz's mother was hospitalised that winter and sadly died within a week. Liz isn't sure how she coped, and reports the commonly felt blur of grief and passing time. 'I still have gaping holes in my memory,' she says:

I became very forgetful and found it impossible to concentrate, so I stopped swimming. Winter swimming is risky and I didn't want to put myself in harm's way. I just couldn't do it. Until one day, my best friend gently encouraged me back to into the icy February water. I screamed and swore like I never had done before, we briefly swam, and then we hopped out. As I got dressed, I realised I now had no one to rush back home to, to prove I was OK. It was just me now. My world was shifting. It felt like a goodbye swim.

I like this idea of the water allowing us to trust ourselves again after the uncertainty that grief hurls at us.

Another swimmer, Rebekah, who was coping with the loss of her mother, also interestingly reported this idea of initial fear of getting back into the sea while coping with grief. She says: 'When my mother died, I found myself coping with an unexpected reaction: I became fearful of things I hadn't been fearful of before. The most surprising thing was that I no longer felt able to swim in the sea.' This subconscious notion of the stability and safeness that our mothers provide us is a really interesting one. When a mother dies, it unsteadies us – our point of reference has gone, and we need to find our own new balance, alone. While many of us may no longer have our mothers (and for some, a mother does not need to have died for the loss of them to be felt), Mother Earth and Mother Ocean can bear witness to our lives – watching, nurturing, present.

The water gives us solace, I think, in its constancy. While it is no replacement for our loss, it is an element that can be healing when we are in or near it. Rebekah's friend encouraged her to come to the sea (again, this need for others to help us to the water appears in many conversations), just to watch her swim, and sit by the waves. 'And slowly, but surely,' she says, 'the sound of the sea lapping the shore, the horizon so far away, the smell of the salt, the feel of the spray all worked their magic, and took the anxiety out of my consciousness. I felt happiest there, peaceful and at ease. I found I could now remember the joy in my lost parents' lives when I was there – rather than feeling the emptiness their deaths brought. I listened to the rhythm of the tides in the moons, and one day I just got back in the water and smiled.'

Sometimes fear and anxiety comes when the water we depend on to make us feel well is taken from us. The coronavirus pandemic of 2020 impacted many bluespace lovers when all public waters were closed for several months worldwide. Despite a re-engagement with natural *green* spaces (for instance, during the one-hour-a-day allocated 'exercise' slot in the UK), many people were bereft at being excluded from water, the spaces that helped them most. One brave woman who spoke to me about this discussed how her obesity had led to various kinds of health problems, which in turn, led to depression and poor self-esteem. She discovered sea swimming and, over time, through being out in nature and the exercise itself, she began to feel better. Remarkably, she cut out or down on a range of medication that she had been dependent on for years. Then – lockdown arrived. Barred from accessing the sea, she began to feel anxious again and her weight crept back on, which made her feel down. And so a negative spiral ensued because her bluespace had been taken away. It was an emotional and difficult story to hear – the rawness and the direct impact of the water on a fragile life. Resolve gained and then lost. Hopefully, she is once more regaining her rhythm. The sea is always there, waiting for us.

So, my advice here is just a gentle encouragement to take yourself to bluespaces as often as you can while coping with fear, loss, anxiety or grief. Allow yourself to feel all your emotions. As I tell children in my ChillSquad classes, you are not your feelings, you just *have* them. So, you are not grief – you are *feeling* loss, you are not useless; you are just *feeling* overwhelmed today, and so on… And all feelings are OK.

EXERCISE
FEELING YOUR GRIEF

Feelings change; they come and go like the weather. Some days, some moments, they overwhelm us, and then they are quiet again for a while. A good practice is to acknowledge them, whatever form they take.

- Try to *name* the feelings you are having (for example, sadness, anger, pain, loneliness, etc.).
- Notice where you are feeling this emotion in your body. (Is it in your heart, your head, stomach, throat or hands, perhaps?)
- Then: stop–pause–breathe – and as you take three deep breaths in and out, imagine *sending kindness to that feeling*, like a white light of energy pulsing through you, to the places in your body and mind where you are experiencing those feelings. Imagine them dissolving away, like melting ice... Keep breathing. This may bring up tears and that's OK. Imagine that you are being your own parent here, allowing the feelings to come up, to witness them with kindness.
- There is a lovely Buddhist saying that very simply whispers: 'I see your suffering, and I am here.' Let us say that *to* ourselves, *for* ourselves now: 'I see your suffering, and I am here.' How does that feel? We can be kind and patient with ourselves as we heal. It's OK.
- Try to practise this when you are walking next to, or getting into, the water. Notice your feelings, name them, feel where they are in your body, send them kindness with your breath, be here for yourself – and let the water take some of these feelings for you.
- Allow yourself also to imagine that the *water* is saying to you, 'I see your suffering, and I am here.'

Space to Heal, Grow and Learn

Sometimes one of the best things we can do when we have come out the other end of a bumpy patch, is to turn inwards and ask ourselves, 'How can I heal from this? How can I recover? Where can I go from here?' Forward movement is a way of not getting stuck in our pain. It's not to say that it goes away, or that what happened/ is happening to us is not valid – just that we can choose, also, if we are able, to move our energy onwards to something positive that helps us. We saw in Chapter 2 that 'keep learning' is one of the recommended Five Ways to Wellbeing. For me, learning is an important value. If we don't *learn* new things, or even discover new ways of seeing what we already know, how can we grow as people? If *we* don't change, then our lives don't change.

I do admit to being a bit of a learning junkie (see Chapter 1!), but I also know that you don't always have to commit to long or arduous paths to learn something new, or to learn about yourself. Learning and growth are about opening our minds. That can happen through conversations, courses and the people we meet. Bluespace encounters give us lots of chances to meet people we might not otherwise come across. I've certainly found that in my own case, with my Salty Seabirds tribe. I've met architects, health workers, midwives, teachers, therapists, yoga and fitness instructors, writers, mothers and more. It is a rich kaleidoscope of experiences and knowledge. We don't usually talk in any depth about what we do – too busy trying not to fall over one-legged in a pair of pants while changing, or chasing a sock down the beach – but even small nuggets can instil ideas and prompt the seeds of change and growth in our own lives.

I've been lucky enough to be asked to speak at various public events on water and wellbeing. It is a wonderful relief to talk with joy and passion at these events without the pressure of competitive academic conferences, where people sometimes try to out-clever each other, or just speak to you for their own networking opportunities. One of the more recent ways that universities are assessing their research 'impact' is to measure how much of it actually reaches the public. What a revelation! All research should do this really, but there is scope too, I guess, for esoteric fancy. All of the public events I've spoken at have had the loveliest audiences, with the best questions – from fellow waterphiles, people who've experienced trauma, women who want to change their life direction and more. When we share our ideas, we are stronger, we learn and we grow.

Sometimes, however, we need to take ourselves away from the busyness of our everyday lives, on our own, so that we can get some perspective on where we are in our lives, what we need, and how to get closer to where we want to be.

FOR THOSE WITH MORE TIME
SOLO RETREAT BY THE WATER

This is something I've been recommending any busy person to do, for years now (especially juggling mothers). I've done it myself every four months for more than ten years – and it is the one thing that really allows you to reset yourself, take stock, breathe, reflect and rest. The beauty of it is that you only need 24 hours.

- If possible, choose a destination no more than one hour's travel from where you live, on or near some bluespace. (A close place means that you don't lose precious time travelling.) Book yourself one night's accommodation, according to your needs and your budget. You can camp, stay in a hostel, Airbnb, find a cheap hotel, or treat yourself to some luxury – whatever works. I travel 50 minutes up the coast from where I live and check into an old faded-grandeur hotel on a seafront; I go to the same place each time because I like the familiarity, and not having to think. You might want to do some research on a few different places and try them out to see what works best for you.
- The key is that you go alone!

- If you have children or work commitments, sort them out on Saturday morning (including cleaning, homework, groceries, etc.) and know that you will be home just after lunch on Sunday to tend to any 'preparations for the week ahead' (such as school uniforms, sports kits, bags, calendars, etc.). Then, give yourself *full permission* to take the next 24 hours for *yourself*. Yes, everyone at home *can* survive that long without you, and this specific Saturday lunchtime to Sunday lunchtime slot is a winning one; I've done it for years so I can report back with full confidence on this one!
- Before you go, buy a nice hardback notebook – one that will become your 'retreat' notebook, or journal. I have one with birds on it, and it makes me smile whenever I see it.
- Pack nightwear, toothbrush, some tea light candles, swim gear, towel, a book, pen, some snacks – and you're good to go. You have nobody to impress when you travel alone; there is great freedom in it.
- Make your way to your destination, check in, absorb your surroundings – breathe, relax and let go. Reassure yourself that you deserve this breathing space, this time to just *be*, and embrace not being in charge of anyone or anything for the next 24 hours. Exhale, and let go of any worries or problems you may be holding inside.
- Now, the fun part... No matter what the weather, go get yourself into the water!
- As you reach the shoreline of whatever bluespace you are in, choose three or four items from nature around you (you can return them to nature at the end of your retreat). These can be pebbles, stones, seaweed, shells, some greenery, leaves, twigs or wildflowers. Whatever you are drawn to. Enjoy this process of choosing your own special items. Put them safely in your bag for later.
- Mindfully and intentionally, notice how you feel and what your breath is doing before you get in and once you are

in. Have a swim, a float, a splash – whatever feels right and safe. Breathe away your other life where you have many responsibilities, and just be *here now* – with yourself, your real self, quiet, inside your mind.

- Let this living water take your worries away, and exchange them for peace, joy, aliveness, and calm.
- When you are finished, get out and either get dressed right away, or wrap up and go back to your accommodation. I'm usually to be seen flying across the road in a hotel brilliant-white towel, dripping all the way back to my room (to disapproving looks) after I get out of the sea!
- Now, if it's an option, run a bath for yourself. Light the tea light candles you brought. Arrange your items from nature which you chose earlier either near the candles or where you will see them once you are in the warm water. Add as many bubbles as you like. Find some nice gentle music on your phone to play. (I'm partial to a bit of rainforest music and the odd 'spa meditation' number!) Or you may just fancy the peace of silence. You choose, it's your retreat. In you go... and relax and luxuriate in the warmth of this water. Notice how different it feels from the water you have just been in. (If you want to do a bath meditation, there is one in the next chapter.) If you are taking a solo retreat in nature and camping, or are in a place with no private bath, you can set up a little meditation space of your own too: just arrange some leaves, flowers, twigs, pebbles, and light a small candle. Allow your body to relax, as per the steps above.
- Then, for the rest of the afternoon or evening, just do whatever you feel like doing. I sometimes nap or mosey around the charity shops for an hour, go back outside and sit by the sea with a coffee... whatever I fancy doing in that moment. No negotiations, no timings, no schedule, no 'when will you be back?', or 'what's for dinner?'. Just you, doing what *you* want to do.

- Then go out for dinner, or make dinner, watch a movie, read your book – again whatever you feel like doing. I usually have another bath before I go to bed, just because I *can*! If you have a favourite body lotion, take that with you and for any future retreats. That way, you will associate the scent with the memory of your restful time alone and it will invoke a sense of peace and purpose in you.
- Now, sleep...
- There is no rush to get up early in the morning, nobody to organise or take care of. Go down for breakfast if you are in a hotel or similar, or make your own if you are not. Take your time. Read the paper, have another coffee or tea. Breathe out any anxiety about being on your own, and choose instead to *relish* it.
- If you want to swim again before or after breakfast, go for it. Another bath or shower may even be in order!
- The final part of your solo retreat is to do some journaling/writing work. There is a lovely old library room in the hotel where I stay, but you can build in time in your room before you check out. I usually check out and then use the library room... or, if it is busy, I find a quiet, open area somewhere in the building. If the weather is nice you can even sit in the garden, or by the water. If you need to tune others out, bring some earplugs.
- Now, having found your space, open your notebook. I recommend writing down three sections:
  1 First, a stream of thought about your 'current life'. Just write from your head: what is going on for you right now, what have you been doing this past six to twelve months? Are you happy, frustrated? Let your emotions come out of your pen.
  2 Next, make some headings such as 'Family', 'Work', 'Relationships', 'Health and Wellbeing', 'Life Purpose', 'Growth' – or anything else that feels relevant to you.

Under each one, make some notes about how satisfied you are about that area of your life, and without overthinking it, write down what you wish for yourself in that area. So, for example, maybe under 'Life Purpose', I might write something such as: 'I'm not all that happy in my job. It was OK for a few years, but I really wish I was doing something in the area of [...] it would feel more like me. I would love a job working with children/I would love to write/to set up my own business' (or whatever it is for *you*). This part of the writing is the dreamlike, no barriers, 'I wish' content... just go for it. What would your ideal scenario be in each category of your life? What would it look like or feel like?

And for the final part:

3   For each subheading you made (or just one or two of them if it seems too much to do all of them), write the subheading title again, but now write down an action plan for what you would like to achieve in the next four months for that theme, when you take your *next* retreat. This needs to be quite specific. For example, 'look up course on start-your-own-business for women on my local council website, and book a place on it within the next eight weeks'. Or, 'find an evening course in creative writing and book it', 'volunteer at a school and send an email to ask for a timeslot', 'investigate a swim-coaching qualification by the end of this month'. The actions need to be specific, and dated... so you don't let yourself off the hook!

Now return to your home, rested, renewed, and with a sense of purpose... part of yourself regained.

Four months later, repeat.

Get the same journal out on the Sunday morning after your swim and rest... and see what has happened in the interim. Did you achieve any of your goals? If not, don't despair; think about what barriers stood in your way and work on them this time round. If you did sign up for things or take action, well done! If you chose two or three areas, can you now focus on another few? As a year or even two passes, you will be surprised to see the gradual shift in your life, more towards how you want it to be!

None of this is a luxury, if that's what you're thinking. These moments of pause and suspension from everyday commitments allow us the space to think and plan what we want from our lives. There is a Dutch concept called *niksen* – a sort of 'doing nothing' practice that entails these ideas of pausing and stillness in order to refresh. We need to feel rested and in the right space, to get quiet within ourselves, so we can really listen to our own inner voice. As a natural setting, bluespace helps to facilitate getting in touch with our own true nature. And we need to do it regularly. Nobody else will make this time and space for you. There is no point in being resentful about never getting to do what you want to do, ahead of meeting the needs of others. *You* are in charge of your own life, so take the time. I promise you will not regret it.

This solo retreat concept has worked for me on many levels. I come home from my 24-hour breaks refreshed, renewed and myself again. Lots of friends say, 'I must come with you next time.' No! The whole point is that you go alone. It is from these moments of retreat that my own life changes have happened. (I've even written an academic paper on 'the need to retreat'!)[1] I've recently started to share this experience by running 'Soul Saturdays by the Sea' mini-retreats in the UK.[2]

Personally, I am also a great fan of doing a course: it moves the energy along in the right direction, even if you don't have time to begin 'the thing itself' right away. And you meet people who can help you. I've come away from my small breaks and booked on to training courses in mindfulness, then children's mindfulness, beach-school and other nature courses. I've loved them all and collectively they've given me the confidence to set up my own enterprises, ChillSquad and WildBlue School, and to run courses and training of my own. Growth, knowledge and a personal sense of purpose that define who we really are, or *want* to be, must begin somewhere. Take some time for yourself to find out what that is for you.

EXERCISE
TAKE A COURSE

This is a really short and simple exercise and can be done as part of your solo retreat, or as a stand-alone practice if you are not taking a retreat.

- Get out a notebook or piece of paper, and write down three areas that you would love to know more about, work in or volunteer in. This could be anything, e.g. writing, art, old people, crafts, archaeology, nutrition, massage, fitness, history, media, surfing or drama.
- Now, look up a short course or two online in your three chosen areas. Your options will naturally depend on your own budget and circumstances. Courses can, however, be taken at weekends, in the evenings, can be one-off/stand-alone, or you can choose small parts

---

or modules of a course that build gradually up into a certificate or qualification, if that is something you want to work towards.

- Make a note of where they are and when they are taking place, e.g. dates, duration, and cost.
- Prioritise which you would like to do most, or first.
- Book it – and just do it!

To grow, we need to give ourselves space and time. When we do this, our personal wellbeing improves. We gradually strengthen our own sense of ourselves, who we are, and why we are here. Water also allows us to feel alive and be ourselves, so I recommend using bluespace to *help* your dreams and hopes emerge.

We've seen here that bluespace helps us in times of need. It is a place of retreat and reflection. As humans, many of us also go to it when we are in emotional, psychological or physical pain. People speak of a *need* to be near water, a longing. At times this draw, this pull, is an almost desperate one. Water is an element unlike any other. It cleanses our spirit, washes away our mental load, even if just temporarily – but we can bathe and bask in it over and over if we need to. The principles and practices of bluespace wellbeing we discussed in Chapter 3 can be called on to help us when we face the sort of challenges that people have shared in their stories in this chapter. Use those principles and practices, and apply them as you need. I have never met a braver tribe than the wild swimmers I've encountered along my way. Our shared stories of pain and hardship are what help to bind us together, in this watery glue of ours.

5

THE CALLING OF THE WATERS

We know by now that water makes many of us feel well, and that research shows this to be true. We have looked, too, at different ways we can engage with water and how we can bring our mind to it through various practices. In addition to these different forms of engagement, there are, of course, many different types of bluespace – outdoor, indoor, everyday and holiday spaces. Whatever our context, all bluespaces offer us something. On days when I am feeling mentally overstretched or frustrated, I find that a windy day by the sea, watching huge waves crash on the shore, helps to clear my mind. On those days when I feel tired, calm water appeals more. I'm sure this is true of many of us – this subconscious matching of mood and personal needs, to water. Let's consider some of these different bluespaces we have in our natural and human environments.

The Sea and Ocean

Water makes up 70 per cent of the earth's surface (freshwater and saltwater combined). That's quite a staggering amount of space! Ninety-seven per cent of that water consists of oceans and seas. These bodies of water are vital not just to our human wellbeing, but to supporting life itself. At the risk of sounding like your old geography teacher, let's pause to consider the water cycle, which is so integral to planetary survival that maybe we can think about its circularity almost as a life lesson in care, time and growth. Water evaporates from the seas and oceans up into the skies, where it condenses and then falls as precipitation (e.g. rain or snow); the freshwater that falls then flows into our lakes and rivers, which, in turn, make their way back to sea level, as water follows gravity and finds its way back to the ocean. And then the cycle starts over: evaporation, condensation, precipitation, transportation, evaporation. As we live our own lives, we too experience cycles: giving up things, weeding out what we don't need, going with the flow of life, sometimes turbulent, sometimes smooth – movement, beginnings and endings. I like to think about water in this way.

My own love of the seas and oceans has deepened over time. I did not grow up by the sea. In fact, I was born in Winnipeg, Manitoba, Canada, prairie country – which may be one of the furthest inland points in the continent of North America! My early childhood was one of outdoor swimming pools and lakes, in searing 40°C heat. We returned to Ireland when I was almost nine years old. Our dad would take us on Sunday drives, to Courtown, County Wexford, the nearest seaside spot, for summer swims. It was usually grey and cold, despite the season. He would swim to the furthest horizon, until we couldn't see him anymore – a small speck in the distance. I remember feeling afraid as I watched him disappear, but he always came back, blue-white skin and shivering with cold, in questionable underwear! And yet these sandy days out sowed a seed of joy. Thirty-six hours before she died, my mother's last outing was to this Wexford beach of our childhood. The last photos we have show her walking along the shoreline, barefoot in the sea. Then, sitting on the rocks, smiling with my father. It was my sister's birthday. Two days later she was gone.

I spoke in Chapter 1 about how the Atlantic Ocean in the west of Ireland helped to heal my soul after her loss. Its wild force matched my own turmoil. Its water took my grief. This solace of the sea and ocean is something so many people can identify with. For a lot of people, it is an urge, or a longing. A woman to whom I spoke for my research observed, 'I need the feel of the water supporting me, the

nature all around, and the tingle of the cold. I've felt quite
desperate for the water at times.' I'm interested in this sense
of almost dependency we have on water, on the fix that the
sea can give us. What is it about getting into a huge body of
saltwater that makes us feel ourselves?

There is, perhaps, a sense of perspective; of huge
horizons and big skies. These also allow us to see our part
in something bigger. One wild swimmer, Catherine C, puts
it beautifully:

*It's the perspective it gives you – I can find myself stressing about
something, then rush to the sea and that enormous stress thing
becomes tiny. I love feeling like a tiny little drop floating in the
vastness. I love swimming away from shore for that very reason –
to find myself floating without edges. My tininess doesn't equate
to nothingness. On the contrary, it makes me feel like an equal and
vital part of one big whole.*

This reminds me of a lovely phrase I came across years ago:
'You are the wave, but so too, you are the ocean.' It is derived
from the words of Paramahansa Yogananda, the Indian yogi,
who said: 'The wave is the same as the ocean, though it is not
the whole ocean. So, each wave of creation is a part of the
eternal Ocean of Spirit. The Ocean can exist without the
waves, but the waves cannot exist without the Ocean.' It has
always stayed with me, this notion of our own lives, problems,
joys – big and small waves at different stage of our life cycles –
yet we are part of something bigger: our community, society,
the planet. I am the wave, yet I too am the ocean. Just so.

When I teach children at my WildBlue School outings, I
always spend some time asking them to describe the sea. An
eclectic mix of responses come shouting back – to do with the
colour of the sea, the waves, the temperature, the beach itself,
creatures, and much more. It is this kaleidoscope of the physical
and the emotional that captures us, I think. Have a think for a
moment about what it is that the sea or ocean does for *you*.

EXERCISE
SEA AND OCEAN MEDITATION

This exercise can be practised when you are at the water or at home, anytime you need the idea of water in order to feel calm. I suggest either reading through the steps first or recording them on your phone, so you can listen to them as you meditate.

- Sitting or lying in a comfortable position, allow your body to relax, and take three deep breaths in through your nose, and slowly out through your mouth. In and slowly out...
- Close your eyes and allow your head and neck to relax; feel your face soften and your jaw loosen.
- Let go of any tension in shoulders, your upper back, your lower back, chest, stomach, arms, hands, legs, and feet... Silently name and then feel each of these parts of your body relax and let go.
- Now, with your eyes gently closed, imagine yourself on a beautiful sandy beach. The sky is blue, the sun is shining and there is a gentle breeze.
- You walk across the soft sand, noticing how this feels on your bare feet.
- You reach the shoreline and feel the cool water touch your toes. Notice how that feels.
- Direct your gaze out to the water, and the horizon. Allow your eyes to soften as you take in the vista before you.
- What colours can you see? What are the waves doing? Imagine them now.
- Listen carefully. Can you hear the sounds of the waves as they meet the shoreline? Are they gently lapping? Are they crashing? Allow the rhythm of this sound to fill your mind for a moment... As the waves come up the beach, breathe in; as the waves drop back, breathe

out. In and out, allow your breath to flow with the waves. In and out...

- Now, notice the smell of the salt air. Breathe it in... Imagine licking your lips and tasting a light covering of salty sea-ness there. Breathe in and out.
- Allow your senses to take in the colours of the sea, the sounds, the smells and taste of it. Relax, let your body soften, and breathe in and slowly out, just noticing how this place looks and feels for you.
- Now, begin to walk again, along the edge of the water. Feel the water and sand at your feet.
- Next, you come to two palm trees, and in the middle hangs a beautiful hammock. Choose what colour or pattern your hammock is, in your mind's eye...
- Gently and easily, get into this hammock, and allow it to hold your body, letting go of any worries or tension.
- Imagine now that one palm tree holding your hammock represents the past and one represents the future. As you breathe in and out, choose now to let go of past worries; they are gone. Breathing in and out, choose also to let go of any future worries you have; they are not here yet. All you need to do is just 'be here now'. Mindfully, in this moment, present. Your hammock, in the centre of these trees, represents the here and now. Fold your hands in your lap, palms upwards, to represent this hammock. Breathe in and out, and silently repeat to yourself, 'just here, now', 'all is well'.
- Take a moment to lie peacefully, here in your hammock, with the sounds and feel of this coastal bluespace around you. Breathe calmly and gently. Just here, now...
- When you are ready, move your hands and feet and open your eyes, adjust your gaze, stretch and yawn if you need to. Come back to the space you are in and take this refreshed, calm feeling with you into whatever you do next.

We've seen already in other chapters how the seas and oceans can help us feel well, through being, doing and connecting with others. All are integral to what wellbeing is about. We can walk next to the sea and drink in its enormity. We can swim in it, play and move on it, or immerse ourselves completely in it. Immersion is one theme that comes up again and again when people are asked what it is that water does for us. Immersion in the seas and oceans cleanses us, heals us, gives us joy, pauses time, makes us forget, makes us remember, connects us to nature and to ourselves.

When researching this book, I asked people a very simple question: 'What does the sea mean to you/do for you?' Responses flowed in and feelings were strong. Salty bluespace has strong resonance with so many of us. Eloise told me how she appreciates, 'The feeling of being separate from the world; being in the sea makes me forget about the chaos of my life, the work and money and parenting. Time stands still and you suddenly remember we are all just a part of nature.' Bill, a lifelong sea swimmer, simply said, 'It's part of my daily routine and it keeps me sane at work.' Nicola noted that, for her, 'Sea swimming has become a coping mechanism for chronic pain and the mental stress that goes along with that. It's the ultimate form of mindfulness, every sense is engaged so you can't think, you can only feel.' This notion of the feelings that the sea can invoke in us came up again for Ellie, who said enthusiastically:

I love the sea, the wild beauty of the surroundings in all weathers. Being in it, engulfed in it, the waves supporting me and lifting me around. The changing seasons, the warm water and the cold. When I'm in the sea, I'm at one with nature and it's a wonderful feeling. Sometimes it just feels wild; sometimes it makes me feel like a big kid, diving into the waves like a seal. I'd been going for two years almost daily and there hasn't been a single time that I didn't love it.

Many of my own swimming friends often declare 'you never regret a sea swim', and it is a simple truth. Once you commit to making that time for it, it never lets you down.

And yet the sea offers much more than fun: for some, it fulfils a wellbeing need that is both important and necessary. Tamsin simply told me: 'Sea swimming has kept me out of hospital for the first winter in five years'. Another man, Phillip, who had been hospitalised with depression several times over the course of five years, said that the cold water was the only thing that made him feel like he was alive when he could not feel his body, or get his body to connect to his mind: 'When I feel low, I feel like my head shuts out my body; I can feel nothing, just a numbness – and the freezing cold water is the only thing that can shock both my limbs and my mind into action again. That's why I don't go in the summer. It doesn't work then.' The research described in Chapter 2 affirms the vital mental health role that water provides for many people.

And even if we cannot always get to it, it holds an important place in our memory stores – I often think back to the best wave I've ever caught (Famara Beach, warm sunshine, azure seas and skies, a perfect left – in case anyone was wondering), or to a magical moment on the beach with friends or family, or a beautiful sunset. These sea memories keep us going when we are unable to get into the sea itself, like a hard drive we can call on when we need it. Emma summarised it well: 'Even saying the words "the sea, the ocean" makes me happy. I don't even need to be there, I can just imagine it straightaway. No other places come to life in my imagination as clearly and easily as the feel and sound and sight of the sea or ocean.' These are powerful words and powerful feelings. The oceans and seas bring us playful joy, friendship, relaxation and nature connection. Whether we are alone or with others, salty bluespace can offer us different things.

EXERCISE
CONNECTION BY THE SEA

This is an exercise for families or groups of like-minded friends. It works especially well if you are away for a day out or on holiday together. It will help you to create bonds with each other and with the coast itself. Read through the steps first, then off you go!

- Set a base camp and mark it with a coat, a stick, or something visible.
- The mission of each member of the family is to do a little beachcomb and come back to base camp with any two items of interest that you find on the beach. Set yourselves a time limit of 15 minutes or so.
- Nominate someone to be the time-keeper, who then calls everyone back if needed. Very young children can team up with a parent. Watch out for changing tides as you set off.
- When everyone returns to base camp with their two items, work as a group to construct a story-space. This will depend on what type of beach you are on. If you are on a sandy beach, you can mark out a square or a circle with sand (perhaps dig a boundary line in the sand with your hands) and decorate it if you like. Or you can arrange some driftwood or logs to make a cosy area... Or you can choose a nook or small cove between some existing rocky outcrops where you will have a space to yourselves. Use your imagination.
- Find a piece of wood, a stone or some seaweed – anything natural really – which will act as the 'talking token'.
- Nominate who will go first; then that person, adult or child, places the talking token in front of them, and begins to tell a story from their imagination, using the first item of their beachcomb treasure!

- When they are finished, the talking token moves clockwise to the next person, who must continue the story, using one of their own items...
- Continue this way until everyone has used their two items (so two turns each) – and then you can either finish, or you can do ad-lib, where whoever wants to verbally add more to the story raises their hand and asks for the talking token, until the story comes to a natural end.
- I've conducted many of these with my own family and with my WildBlue School groups – children love it! – so here's a quick example of how this might sound:

  - ❑ The first person holds up a piece of driftwood and begins: 'Once on a very stormy night, a pirate boat was shipwrecked on the rocky coast of Cornwall [or insert where you are]. It splintered into many pieces, and this driftwood was part of it.'
  - ❑ The talking token moves to the second person, who holds up a small shell and says, 'The pirates were searching for this shell, which has magic powers...'
  - ❑ Then the next person holds up a crab leg and continues: 'When the shell is rubbed, it makes everything fly/grow bigger/grow smaller' [use your imagination!] – like this crab, Charlie, who grew to the size of a small horse and now protects this beach day and night.'

And so on! You may need to play a few rounds to get into the swing of this game, if it is new to you. Or you can do it a few times during your holiday. The suggestion 'let's do a beachcomb story' usually makes everyone happy – and you can do it in all kinds of weather too. If you are allowed to, you can add a small campfire to add that something extra, for evening stories. It is a great way to get people talking to each other and working together.

The sea *means* so much to so many of us. It is more than a body of water. It is a place where we can be ourselves, where we can have fun with and connect to ourselves and others, make memories and calm our minds. It holds deep psychological space for us as humans. And for that reason, it is like no other place on earth. All 70 per cent of it.

Rivers and Streams

On Irish summer childhood days, when the 35-minute drive to sea wasn't an option, my parents would sometimes take us to nearby rivers to swim. This was joyful, freshwater freedom. One river we went to was accessed across two fields, only visited by those in the know. The other ran swift and fierce, under an arched ancient stone bridge at Aghade, and was often used for kayak slalom racing. Bored senseless in our long Irish summer holidays, pre-internet, we kids aged ten and eleven would often cycle the six miles to that river, and spend the day there alone and unsupervised. We threw sweets from the bridge while the others dived for them, we rock jumped and swam for hours, eating a picnic lunch, only returning at dusk. There were no mobile phones, no timeframes or worries, really. It didn't cross my mind that one of us might drown or get into difficulty. (However, please do heed the safety note at the start of this book when you are wild swimming!) The only thing we thought about was the water and the fun to be had in it.

Rivers evoke these lovely childhood memories for me in lots of ways. In Winnipeg as children, we had the Assiniboine River. It was so cold there, in the centre of the continent, that the river would freeze over completely in the winter. People would ice skate and walk along it, as if it were just another routeway in the city. It's hard to imagine such a force of nature, a giant river, being frozen and stopped in its tracks by another force of nature – the weather. One of my favourite programmes growing up was a British kids' nature-story programme called *Tales of the Riverbank*. It was an utter delight – Hammy Hamster and his little friends, who lived by the river, going on adventures in miniature boats and playing with sticks and leaves. I can still hear the theme tune in my mind, all these years later. Many of you will have read the *Wind in the Willows* and other nature/creature stories where rivers feature. What is your favourite one, I wonder?

I find rivers mesmerising. Watching the water flow past, while wondering where it has been and where it is going, puts me in a state of wonder – a daydream almost. I asked some wild swimmers what it is about rivers, per se, that drew them in. Andy said, 'My preference is the river - it's my own little bit of heaven. Although it's public, once I'm in the water in the summer I can't be seen due to the growth of nettles, etc. on the bank. Over the last ten years I really only ever see dog walkers.' So, perhaps there is more solitude in the river for some? A busy summer beach is fun in many ways, but certainly not peaceful, if that's what your mind needs.

Kate, who lives in the Scottish Highlands, said that for her the colour of the river is something special:

I think these peaty browns and hazel hues are gorgeous to watch. There is nothing quite like looking at a moving river. I would never swim in one (I'm too scared of fish, and currents!), but I could sit by one and just watch a river all day long. I prefer rivers to the sea. You've got trees and greenery all around you. You can hear the birds sing, and watch the insects. When the sun shines on a river, you get this dappled light on the surface. It's just beautiful.

One of the things I love about water is how much it changes depending on the weather and where it is going. If you are able to follow a river along its course for example, you can notice all kinds of changes in it. Fast flowing water that eddies through moss-covered rocks – rushing forward in haste. Then, the lower reaches, where the river matures and wanders, calmer, wider, with an even water flow. I am very tempted to break into a full-on geography lesson here on fluvial geomorphology – V-shaped valleys, meanders and ox-bow lakes – but you can find that in your old schoolbooks! What I want us to ponder is the way a river or stream makes us feel. What do you think of when you see one? Does it make you want to get into it? Swim or paddle? Or get a kayak out and rush downstream with it? Does it encourage you to walk alongside it, or to sit and gaze at it?

There is a wonderful book called *How to Read Water* by Tristan Gooley.[1] In it, he talks about all the different forms of water we come across in nature. I love this book because it appeals to my inner geographer and aquaphile on every level! His chapter on rivers and streams includes a section called 'riffles, pools, glides, and other delights'. To me, this is like a chocolate box of natural enchantments. He writes wonderfully about the changing shapes and movement of rivers, their flora and fauna, and seasonality. I think a river, stream, or even canal bank walk encapsulates this notion of change. Change, as we walk longitudinally along it, with a start and end point; but also change of seasons and vegetation. We can note easily when certain trees or flowers are in leaf or bloom, and where we can stop for shade or shelter when we walk by these bodies of moving freshwater. They invite us to move with them. Walking in a shallow stream (carefully and wearing wellies if necessary) can be a lovely thing to do too, and gives a completely different perspective of the water.

There is a sense of peace to be found in walking by rivers too that improves our wellbeing. One New Yorker, Monica, told me that she always walked home from work by the Hudson River, just so she could let go of her day, even though it added an extra ten minutes to her journey. 'It's the one thing I really look forward to, after my work day,' she said, 'just getting on my coat and walking down to that river path. I love the smell of the river and seeing how high the water is on any one day. Walking along beside it makes me let go of my work stuff, so by the time I get home I am ready to be mom again'. Rivers are valued in so many ways. House prices by rivers are higher, fishermen sit and enjoy their banks and bounty, and of course, in times past, they were the central points of transportation and settlement.

Most of our major world cities are traversed by rivers. Most major settlements began around them. And these rivers are the arteries, the soul of many urban spaces. When I am at work in London and the commute has been long, or the workday draining, I take myself to sit by the Thames and watch the water, to restore my balance. I watch the pleasure boats, the freight barges, the commuter catamarans – all going about their business. I noticed the tide changes and the colour of the water. I often imagine what is happening in all the apartment buildings stacked alongside its banks, the lives of the inhabitants, as they too look out onto this same river. I think back to the days of river transport, where the Thames was the heart of London's docklands, its banks a hive of warehousing and trade activity,

Rivers also hold spiritual significance in many cultures. The Ganges in India, for example, is regarded as sacred water. Winding 1,560 miles across northern India, from the Himalaya Mountains to the Indian Ocean, the Ganges River is a sacred entity. Known as 'Ganga Ma' – Mother Ganges – the river is revered as a goddess whose purity cleanses the sins of the faithful and aids the dead on their path toward heaven. Bathing corpses of the dead may perhaps invoke shudders in Western cultures, but in India this is a sacred ritual. Hindu belief, in particular, holds that bathing in the river before any festivals and after death is a form of purification, causes the forgiveness of transgressions and helps the soul to attain salvation. Bathing the bodies of the dead in the Ganges is thought to bring the souls of the deceased closer to freedom and enlightenment. So, this symbolism is central to the cultural value and spiritual wellbeing of those who honour it. And let's remember that wellbeing does involve the spirit for many people – not just the body and mind, as we saw in Chapter 2. Water and ritual play a role in this spiritual wellbeing. In Ireland, we talk about giving someone 'a good funeral' – the sense that person lost to us was given a proper send-off, where our cultural traditions are adhered to and honoured. This gives families a sense of comfort later, in their grief. The Ganges River ritual is part of a watery spiritual practice that gives peace to people too.

But like the sea, rivers can be treacherous. Earlier in this book, I recounted my near-death tale of drowning in the Zambezi River – so I have a healthy respect for fast moving freshwater! Rivers can be dangerous not just for sports and swimming, but because of their potential to flood and devastate all around them. In many parts of the world, people build homes on flood plains because space is in short supply. We've seen so many disasters around river flooding – causing huge damage to life and property. This cyclical destruction shows us not only the negative climate effects we are having on the earth, but also the power of water and how *it* rules us, not the other way around. Respect for water and the force of nature is something we always need to remember, whenever we engage with bluespaces. We can swim in rivers, kayak or paddleboard down them, fish in them, sit and watch them, or walk alongside them. All bring their own joy and wellbeing.

EXERCISE
MINDFUL WALKING FOR THE RIVERSIDE

This can be undertaken at any river, stream or canal, as part of your everyday week or on holiday and daytrips. Read through the steps beforehand.

- Make a mindful intention that for five or ten minutes of your walk, you will deliberately try to notice your breath, your body and your surroundings – with peaceful, non-judging presence.
- Take three deep breaths in and out. Close your eyes momentarily and let go of any tensions from your day, and from your mind.
- Begin walking, and as you do, notice the fall of your footsteps on the ground beneath you. How does your body feel as it walks like this? What is your breath doing? Notice the pace you are choosing – just observe it, and breathe in and out.
- Notice now the ground beneath your feet: is it clay, mud, wet, dry, paved or natural? What you can you tell about the shape and feel of this pathway? Just label it in your mind, resisting the urge to critique it; for example, 'a grassy overgrown path' or 'a muddy, slippery track' – and breathe in, breathe out, breathe in, breathe out. How are your feet moving on this path? Give gratitude for the gift of feet that can walk and a body that can move, here, now, in this moment.
- Now as you walk, cast your gaze to the water itself. What colours can you see? What is the surface of the water doing? Is it moving slowly, or quickly? Are there eddies, whirlpools, currents – bubbles on the top?

- Can you see any other features in the river or by its banks? Rocks, branches overhanging, trees, reeds, shrubs or undergrowth? Look closely, with curiosity, naming what you can see silently in your mind's eye.
- Now stop for a moment. Notice your breath. Let it regulate and slow down. Now listen. What can you hear? Birds, insects? Traffic? Humans? Just notice each sound, without judgement.
- Carry on walking, and this time see if you can combine noticing your breath and your body as it walks on the surface beneath you, with taking in the sounds of the landscape and the movement and colours of the flowing water beside you. Combined together, be present in this bluespace and allow its beauty and its own sense of itself – flowing regardless of what you are doing or thinking – to bring you peace and calm.
- When you finish your walk, end with a few deep breaths, give thanks to the water, and wish it well on its way. This same body of moving water will never pass in front of you again. Or, as Heraclitus, the Greek philosopher said, 'No man ever steps in the same river twice, for it is not the same river and he is not the same man.' (Or, indeed, woman!)

Rivers and streams can teach us a lot about our own wellbeing. They give us a sense of peace and of freedom. There is a lovely Irish folk song my mother loved called 'Only Our Rivers Run Free', which is a truth in itself. We can try to manage, divert and subjugate rivers, but ultimately water will find its own way – always searching for freedom, and its own course. There is much we can learn from this as a metaphor for life.

Ponds

Unlike the showy ostentation of a wild, rushing river, a pond is usually a peaceful and quiet place. Often small and surrounded by vegetation, ponds are sometimes man-made, sometimes natural – but many people hold a unique fondness for them. Maybe this is because they are often the only form of available bluespace for many people who live inland or in cities? They sit, often, in the heart of a village or a city with lots of natural vegetation surrounding them, and a bench or grassy bank, encouraging contemplation and reflection.

Many people build ponds in their own garden and watch the plants change with the seasons, small fish, tadpoles and wildlife come and go. Being near to or having a pond in your own space allows you to connect with nature in a very gentle way.

One of my favourite watery books is called *At The Pond*, by a collection of women writers.[2] This is an account of human interactions at the women's bathing pond on Hampstead Heath in London. The editor takes a seasonal approach, dividing the book into four sections, and includes accounts of a number of women's relationships with the pond across a calendar year. It is a real delight to read and instantly made me want to catch the train to London and swim in the ponds. This urban bathing place is home to lots of wildlife, varieties of fish and birds and insects galore. But what is really interesting is this interaction between the women who use the pond, the water itself and the community of fellow swimmers. Nina Powles acknowledges the importance of this place in her chapter, 'Small Bodies of Water', writing, 'I suddenly feel like I have reached a sacred place that is part of so many women's lives. The sunlit pond is fringed with reeds and willows, and tiny blue dragonflies skim about the surface. Lowering myself down from the platform at the edge, I launch myself into the water.' There is an acknowledgement throughout this book of the acceptance of aged bodies, of the wisdom and carelessness about image that being in this bluespace brings. Respect and honour are implicitly given to the stoics – those who swim all year, no matter what the British weather is throwing at them. There is a sense of ritual, the repetition of a practice integral to lives and wellbeing. A needed place.

In her chapter, 'A Quietening', Sophie Mackintosh speaks of the value of a quiet water space in a busy city like London. She notes that the pond itself allows for a recovery of sorts from the city. There is this juxtaposition, this reciprocity – of take and give, give and take, crazy and calm. Sometimes, she says, she feels like London can chew you up, but also put you back together. After a big night out on the town, the water gives salvation! In the pond, Mackintosh says, '…everything fades away: expensive taxis, corner-shop wine purchased at 3am, taking the tube home in the morning dressed in last night's clothes, while swigging from a bottle of water. There is no better hangover cure, me and my friends agree. No better forgiveness. No better permission to be still.' I think this is wonderful: a real-life account of a young woman's city existence, busy, fun, extrovert, set alongside the peace and introverted calm of the pond. And who is to say that watery recovery from a Big Night Out isn't as valid a form of wellbeing as the next?

Of course, there is a men's pond at Hampstead Heath too, and a mixed bathing pond. But many have spoken of the freedom they find in being with their own gender, an ease of swimming, changing, and a lack of body consciousness. The wellbeing benefits of the pond are similar to many bluespaces: cold water immersion in winter and spring, physical exercise, a time to pause daily worries, companionship and camaraderie for those who want it, and, perhaps, the constancy of a natural bluespace as a place of refuge.

EXERCISE
POND-RIPPLE KINDNESS

This is a very simple and easy exercise that is an adaptation of the Buddhist loving-kindness practice. However, you don't need to be a Buddhist or to have heard of this practice before; it's just a lovely wellbeing exercise. If you wish, read through this exercise first and then keep the steps in mind as you do it. (As you will see, it's best to do it at a place where there are no swimmers!)

- When you next go to a pond, take with you three small stones or pebbles, or find them there.
- Take a seat on the grass or a bench near the water's edge.
- Hold a pebble in your hand (just the one for now, place the other two on the ground or in your pocket) and close your eyes for a moment. Notice the feel and texture of the pebble, as you take three deep breaths, in and out. As you exhale, consciously try to let go of any worries that you have in your life right now.
- Open your eyes again and cast your gaze to the surface of the pond. Notice the water – its colour, its movement and the sky above it, whilst also keeping your attention on your breath, softly breathing in and out normally.
- Now, as you watch the water, think of someone you love and admire in your everyday life. It can be a parent, partner, friend or someone else. Close your eyes for a moment and imagine that person in your mind's eye. As you breathe in, allow your heart to fill with love for that person. As you breathe out, silently say to yourself, 'I wish you kindness.'

- Open your eyes and throw the pebble in your hand into the pond. Notice the ripples it makes on the water. As you notice this, think of all the good and kind things this person does for you and for others. Take a big breath in and out, appreciating this person for all they do, and all they are (even if you don't always show them this).
- Take the second pebble in your hand, close your eyes, and think of the whole earth, bluespaces, rivers, lakes, ponds and oceans – all of nature. Notice what images come to mind. Breathe in, and as you do, imagine your heart filled with love for this earth, this nature, this water. Breathe out and silently say: 'I wish you kindness and care.'
- Open your eyes and throw the second pebble into the pond. Notice the ripples it makes on the water. As you notice this, think of all the good things this earth, this water, does for you and for others, the joy, the peace it brings. Take a big breath in and out, appreciating this earth, this nature, and this water.
- Take the final pebble in your hand, close your eyes, and connect now to your own self. If it helps, you can gently and silently greet yourself, e.g., 'Hello, Catherine!' or 'Hello, you!' Notice your body, your feelings and your thoughts. How are they today, in this moment? Breathe in, and as you do, imagine your heart filled with love and kindness for yourself. Breathe out, and silently say to yourself: 'I wish you kindness.' You can repeat this a time or two if you find it hard. This step can bring tears and that's OK – often we are not used to directing our love and kindness to ourselves, so it can feel strange. But it is important.
- Open your eyes and throw the last pebble into the pond. Notice the ripples it makes on the water. As

you notice this, think of all the good things you do for others in your life, especially the small everyday things. You can silently name them in your mind (for example: looking after my family/parents, walking my dog, being a friend/good colleague, taking out the rubbish, sharing my food, listening). Take a big breath in and out, appreciating yourself, with kindness and gentleness, here on this earth, beside this water.

You can do this practice with the same people, different people, people you love, people you need to forgive, friends, family, partners, and yourself. The ripples of the pond show us the effects that kindness has. Our breath connects us to ourselves, to the water, and the mindful intention of kindness. To offer kindness brings us peace inside. The stillness of a pond facilitates and reflects this possibility for peace.

Lakes

Lakes have always had a mysterious and enigmatic quality, I think. From tales of Scotland's Loch Ness Monster to the poetry and paintings of the British Lake District and the Great Lakes of North America, these freshwater pockets have much to offer. Countries like Switzerland are famed for their lakes – and their (usually glacial) waters create leisure and wellbeing centrepieces for many towns and cities in an otherwise hemmed-in country.

I visited my dear friend, Dawn, in the Swiss city of Lucerne recently – as land-locked as you can get – and found myself feeling a bit geographically–psychologically claustrophobic. (Does anyone else suffer from that, I wonder? When being too far inland makes you a bit nervous?) It was November, and the jagged mountains surrounding this picture-postcard place were snow-capped and very, very high. In a bid to throw off that slightly choked feeling, I donned my swimsuit as soon as I could and got into the icy (3°C) waters of Lake Lucerne. Not a soul around, just a few bemused looks from passing local Swiss folk, warmly clad in duck-down jackets, hats and scarves. There was a still beauty, quite unique, to floating alone in such a beautiful body of freshwater while looking up at the snowy mountains. It was relaxing not to have to think of tides, currents, waves or even the depth.

Many people love the uniqueness that lakes have to them, a combination of freshness – fresh water, and fresh air. One woman, Karen, observes what it is she loves about lakes: 'It's the feeling of the cold water on my face. The *smell* of the cold water close to my face. It's like clean, line-dried washing in the Lake District. The views you can only see from the middle of the lake. And many more wonderful things.' I asked Karen what it was about lakes in particular that made them different to swimming or being in other types of bluespace. She replied, 'It can get very busy in the Lake District but when you're in the water it's so peaceful, quiet and calming. I always think about the water running straight off the mountains, clean, fresh and clear. You have no choice but to be mindful, because in this water you are just being, present, there.'

I think the idea of being contained is sort of comforting too – there is a finite perimeter to a lake. You may not always be able to see all of it from where you are, but you know it is there. I think at certain times in our life, our week, even our day, we feel the need to be held; and at others, the wide expanse of an ocean or sea, a big horizon without limits, gives us freedom and solace. This changing relationship between the topography, the geography of water and our own emotional and physical needs is fascinating.

Bill's Story

My own love of lakes comes from growing up near Lake Huron, Michigan, one of the five 'Great Lakes' in the USA – although the border between Canada and the US runs right through the water of each lake (except Lake Michigan); how cool is that? For me, the lake is a place to swim in, take my boat out on, and to go fishing on. When I was a kid, my family home was right on the water. We had a small wooden jetty you could sit on. One of my earliest memories is dangling my feet over the edge of it. In fact, all my good childhood memories involve the lake. My dad showed me how to run his small boat, how to fish and how to swim there. My friends and I would hang out there all summer. As an adult, I moved further away, to Chicago, but still not far from the lakes.

I quit my job about five years ago due to overload and stress burnout. I was managing a big sales team for an IT company and it all just got too much. The push to bring in more business, more money, more people – just 'more', all the time. I was working late every day, barely seeing my family and catching up on even more work at weekends. I didn't know how to hit the stop button. Men are supposed to just keep going, right?

Then one day my body stopped for me. I ended up in the hospital with a bleeding ruptured ulcer. St Joseph's Hospital had a view of Lake Michigan and as I lay there in recovery, I had time to look out my window at the water and reflect on this crappy lifestyle I had got sucked into. Looking at the lake reminded me of my childhood at Lake Huron. Life was simple then. I thought to myself, if I can get off this treadmill then life could be like that again. I know it sounds corny, but I did have one of those lightbulb moments you see in the movies. I was heading straight for an early grave, with the high-pressure life I was living. For what?

So, I quit my job, moved my family out of the city to Cheboygan, back on the banks of Lake Huron. I now work as a freelancer from home and we swim in the lake and hike the trails of the state park we live by. It's back to nature, and back to the water. I've started lake swimming again and got myself a little boat that I take my own son out on. I'm grateful for the wakeup call, in all honesty. A life by the water keeps you in touch with what matters.

There are many cultural connotations associated with lakes. The Celts in Ireland and Scotland built crannógs – wooden houses and small settlements on islands in the middle of lakes. They were used as protective places for people and their livestock to live, fortified against potential invaders. Recreated versions can still be visited in heritage centres today. In South America, Lake Titicaca in Bolivia is the world's highest altitude navigable lake. It holds the mystery of the Inca peoples and their ruins are still there today. Chincana is a ruined Incan settlement on a small island within the lake. It bears testimony to the ancient history of the lake as an important trading place across the body of water. Many South American native tribes believed that deities resided in their lakes and would make sacrificial offerings of gold and jewels into the water as part of seasonal rituals. Now Lake Titicaca is an important tourism destination, a bucket-list checkpoint for South American travels. The ancient and the contemporary exist side by side in this unique bluespace.

Lakes are life-sources too, where freshwater is scarce. Physical wellbeing depends on the most basic human need: water to drink. Lake Victoria, for example, is the largest lake in Africa and the chief reservoir for the River Nile. Millions of people in Tanzania, Uganda and Kenya depend on it for water supplies just to survive. Interestingly, despite being such an important resource for life, Lake Victoria is also seen as one of the most dangerous lakes in the world. The weather can be extreme and unpredictable there, with patchy communication signals, accompanied by water of extremely varied depths.

This fear of unknown depths in lakes seems to be a common one. As a child, I often heard adults say 'never swim in a lake, they are full of holes'. There are superstitions and stories around lakes, of people being drowned never to be seen again. As a geographer, I know that all geomorphological features can be explained and mapped, but it is interesting to see the label of mysteriousness that is given to lakes by many people. In times past, there were many fearful superstitions associated with lakes by tribal people. First Nations people hold many beliefs about lakes. They were often thought to be places occupied by ghosts and evil spirits. The Chibchas in Colombia in South America would throw precious things into the lakes to appease the spirits they believed were there.

Near my own birthplace, Lake Winnipeg (which we thought *was* the sea, as children, because it was so huge and had a sandy shore), there are also many First Nations' superstitions. Many limestone caves are found along the western shore of the lake, and the Indian peoples traditionally believed that malignant fairy people resided in them and the waters nearby. If they came across one of these caves when they were out hunting and fishing along the lake, they would either give it a wide berth, or they would get out of their canoe and lay an offering on the beach, to respect any spirits there. I guess we can all ponder on what it takes for us to feel well and safe as humans, across time and space, when it comes to lake water. The mysteries of the deep.

EXERCISE
LAKE WATER CLEANSE

This is a very simple exercise which connects the ideas of cleansing and letting go with immersion in freshwater. Read it through before you enter your lake.

- Dress in your preferred swimwear and, when you are ready, take a moment to stand at the edge of the lake before you even touch the water. (Keep your towel or robe on at this point if it's not a warm day.)
- Close your eyes for a moment, and take three deep breaths in and out...
- And now call to mind something you need to let go of in your mind or your life – such as a worried thought that is nagging at you, an over-rumination of a past conflict or interaction, a relationship, or any pain that you are having, physical or otherwise... There may be a few things for you to consider, so try to prioritise! You can always repeat this exercise on your next swim with another worry.
- Now open your eyes, and gently walk into the water. Notice mindfully the temperature of it, the feel of the water on your skin. What are your body and your breath doing in response? Observe and be with it... regulate your breathing as you need to... remembering to exhale long and slow...
- When you are safely in the water at chest depth and still able to touch the bottom of the lake, cast your gaze to the surface of the water and the sky. Breathe in and out, and give gratitude for this place. A simple 'thank you for this beautiful place' will do.
- Bring the issue you need to let go of to mind now, and as you do, hold your breath (and hold your nose too if you prefer!) and dunk your head under water for the count of three – allowing the water to take this problem from your mind. Come back up to the surface and exhale the feelings associated with that problem away...
- Repeat this once more: inhale in, hold your breath, dip under for three seconds, and this time silently repeat to yourself before/during your dunk: 'Problem/worry be gone, I release you into the water.' (Examples might be:

'Hurt from my argument with Jack, be gone, I release you into the water'; 'Friend-betrayal be gone, I release you into the water'; 'Aching lower back, be gone, I release you into the water'; 'Migraine be gone, I release you into the water'; 'Headful of lists and schedules be gone, I release you into the water in this moment', or a simple 'Grief, be gone, I release you into the water'.) It's important to use your own words, those that feel congruent to you, as these words are the ones that will make helpful neural pathways in your brain (see Chapter 2).

- By linking, or 'anchoring' as the psychologists call it, an intention with a habit or action, we are more likely to remember to do it. If you are feeling bad about something, stressed or in pain, you can try this exercise anytime, so that you relate the cleansing power of freshwater with a release of something that you need to let go of.

Note: You can also do this exercise in your shower: just think of what you need to release – and, for maximum effect, instead of dunking for three seconds, you can switch the shower to cold water for three seconds instead, to blast the pain away, metaphorically.

Waterfalls

Is there anything as majestic as a waterfall? Waterfalls sum up the roaring power of water, in vertical, linear form. Of course, there are different types of waterfalls; there are the gentle, lower river-reach waterfalls, tumbling over mossy rocks in wide meandering water. Then, in the upper reaches of a river, where water carves its course downhill with gravity, we can find the awe-inspiring waterfalls that drop from great heights, cascading down into pools and canyons below. Their sheer force creates these pools below, where the water gouges out the rock floor underneath, holding briefly the overspill from above before it continues its journey.

When we watch a waterfall we are drawn in to the awe of it. As well as the huge compulsion to take photographs of it, we are often silenced by the wonder of a waterfall. Where did all this water come from? Where is it going? The sensory assault of the *sound* of a waterfall makes us remember how powerful the earth is and how small we really are in comparison. I've walked along the edge of Victoria Falls in Zimbabwe, soaked in the spray and mist from the sheer force of water. I actually slipped badly on some wet rock right on the edge of the falls – no fences anywhere in sight, and thought, wow, how simple it would be to fall and die, just like that.

Despite having seen some very impressive waterfalls around the world, one of my very favourites are the Glenariff waterfalls, in the glens of Antrim in Northern Ireland. This is a beautiful green, unspoilt part of the world, where my mother grew up and where my extended family still live. Glenariff is a stunning U-shaped glaciated valley, with typically high sides and a low valley bottom that extends to the sea. It's a myriad of patchwork green fields and hedgerows. I go there every year to visit family, but last year I took the plunge, for the first time, and got into a waterfall to swim. I won't deny it, I was quite nervous – echoes of lakes and waterfalls having holes and the stories of them 'dragging people in' flitted across my mind briefly. It was 7am on a cold Irish spring morning. This waterfall lies within the most beautiful forest you can imagine, full of every kind of tree, wildflowers, ferns, birdlife and rare red squirrels. The smell is of earth, mulch and rich fresh air. I approached the muddy path down to the waterfall through a canopy of dappled greens, and of course I could hear it before I saw it.

And there it was, rushing, tumbling white water, flowing into a dappled brown but clear-water pool below. Not huge – medium-sized I would say, as waterfalls go. But in that moment, it was all mine – a world apart. I climbed over the wooden fence and laid my gear down on a flat rock, pulled on my swim shoes for grip, and gingerly eased into the cold water. And by GOD, it was cold! Once I caught my breath, I went a little deeper, and then strove out, towards the impact zone of the waterfall. What bliss, what sound, what cold, what a feeling! I will never forget that experience, of being one with nature, in an ancestral place. My beloved Aunt Mary, who has a healthy fear of water, almost did have a heart attack when I told her where I had been that morning. 'It just isn't something people do there,' she insisted. She had never heard of it. 'Why would you *do* such a thing?' she asked, worried and puzzled. Why wouldn't I? I just had never thought of being *in* that waterfall before. Now I can't wait to go back and do it again.

Try This

I'm not giving a longer exercise for waterfalls because most of us (unless you are very lucky) don't live near one. They are special watery treats for trips and holidays.

But when you are next at one, try to take a moment of quiet. Even if there are others around you, and your hands are twitching to take pictures, tune all of this out for a moment. Take three deep breaths in and out, and allow yourself to become still. Very simply, cast your gaze to the movement of the water. Look at the point of contact where the water 'tips over' the precipice, and notice the smoothness of that point. Notice next the width and height of the rushing water as it falls and crashes below. Absorb the power of that – and take it into your own heart and mind. Focus on the following anchor thought: *waterfalls are power and strength.*

Allow yourself to feel the courage and strength of the waterfall. Is there something in your life that needs this power right now? If so, breathe in the force of this water, and let it guide you in what you need to do. Then notice, too, the calmer water that flows after the powerful surge – what is happening downstream of the waterfall you are looking at? Often, we get peace from taking powerful action in our lives, a strong but quiet resolve.

Other Types of Bluespace

There is no doubt that nature gives us many wonderful bluespaces to engage with – coastal, inland, salty, freshwater, big, small and everything in between. But sometimes we can't get outside to be in them. We might not live close to them, or we may not have the time to go as often as we want to, even if we do have bluespaces nearby. The weather can put us off, as can nobody else being free to join us, not being sure how or where to start, or even just our own moods and fatigue. Some days all we can manage is our journey to work and back. Some days, it can just be too hard to even leave our homes. And that's OK. But we don't have to forfeit the wellbeing benefits of water, even then. Let's consider some of the everyday, non-wild versions of bluespace that can help us.

Baths

You hear people say 'I'm a bath person', or 'I'm more of a shower person'. I often wonder where that comes from. Maybe some of us like to feel immersed in water, and other prefer to feel it rushing over us. Maybe it's just a time and expediency thing, or a cultural one? I have never seen my partner take a bath, not once, in all the years I have known him. But for me, a bath is one of life's greatest pleasures. On a cold evening, returning home after a commute, or a stressful day at work – kids fed and bedded – the bliss of sinking into warm deep water is a great way to let go of your day.

EXERCISE
MINDFUL BATHING RELAXATION

Immersion in warm water cleanses us, relaxes our body and mind and encourages us to let go of what has just been. Baths are not for everyone, but they can help us lots when we can't get outdoors. It's a good idea to read through the exercise below first, or record it to listen to while you are soaking in your bath.

- Gather a couple of natural items that you are drawn to. I use pebbles, small pieces of driftwood, seaweed, shells, twigs, flowers, leaves or grasses. (You can return these to nature afterwards, if you wish.)
- Run the water to your own preferred temperature and add in bubble bath, Epsom salts, and/or aromatherapy oils (three or four drops of lavender, rose or geranium are good).
- Light two candles at the front of your bath, where you can see them. (Tea lights will do!)
- Arrange your items near your candles. (Please take great care not to set anything on fire!)
- Start some meditation music on your phone (choose this earlier, so you don't spend time deciding at this moment). Set your phone to silent so you won't be disturbed by incoming calls or messages. Close and lock the door, if necessary, so you won't be disturbed by anyone else in your household.

- When you are all set, get undressed and prepare to let a warm bath offer you watery relaxation.
- Take a deep breath. Stand for a moment, before you get in. Without judgement, acknowledge the sensation of your own unclothed body in the air. Ground your feet, and choose to 'be in your body' just for a moment. Close your eyes and notice the temperature of the room, and how your body feels. Is it tired, tensed, heavy, light, relaxed or stressed? Can you feel where in your body any particular aches or stresses are showing up? Take another deep breath and send that breath to those parts of your body. Open your eyes, breathe in and out.
- Now, as you are about to enter the water, say silently to yourself, 'I am moving into the water' – and then, gently get in.
- Notice your own initial response to the water. What is your breath doing? Are you holding it? Breathe. Acclimatise to the temperature, and this new sensation – of being wet, submerged, or partially submerged.
- You may feel the urge to adjust the water depth or temperature. If so, do it now.
- Then, just relax and let go.
- Allow your body to sink into the water... letting go of any worries, or any thoughts that you do not need, in this moment.
- Notice how your body now feels, compared to how it felt just before you got into the water.
- What words can you bring to mind to describe this?
- Breathe in, and breathe out – slowly, gently, deeply, three times. Close your eyes now, and notice this new feeling of being in warm water.
- As you relax, allow the water to take your worries and thoughts away...

- You don't have to, but if it feels right for you, hold your breath, close your eyes and allow your head, face and hair to dip momentarily under the water. Come back up and wipe the water from your face. Allow your day to be taken away and dissolved by the water. If you like, you can do this two or three times.
- Focus now, only on your own breath – not controlling it, just noticing it.
- You may wish to direct your gaze to your candles... breathing in and out...
- And then to your pieces of nature: really try to notice their colours, their textures, size, shape, and think about where they came from – how they grew or came to be... with gratitude and wonder, for each small item and all it took for that nature to be with you, in this moment.
- Breathing in, and out... close your eyes and send thoughts of gratitude to your mind – for clean, warm running water instantly coming from your tap, in this home, this shelter. Water that you did not have to carry, or fight for, or decontaminate; water that you can access daily, in this way...
- Allow your body to connect with this water now... quietly, in gratitude, with your breath...
- When you are ready, unplug the plug, and visualise your worries gently swirling away as the water disappears.
- After you get out and dry off, pay attention to how your body feels after being in the water, and know that you can retain or access this feeling of warmth and calm anytime you choose to.

Showers

In Chapter 2 we looked at Wim Hof's work on cold water therapy – and cold showers play an important role in his ideas. The 'Iceman' is a firm believer in blasting our body to rebalance our wellbeing. In that chapter we talked about the science of cold-water wellbeing. A shower is another way of literally washing away our day if we take one in the evening. And if we take one at the start of a day then it wakes our body up from slumber and kick-starts our mind, ready for action.

Yet we have become picky, in the West, about the quality of our showers. Many of us like strong, forceful power showers, with multiple jets perhaps. Some showers even come with lighting and piped music. But, if we strip away the basics, we can think about the wonder of a jet of water in our home that we can control – that we can switch on and off whenever we choose, and make warmer or colder, stronger or more gentle. It is amazing if we think of it. If you have ever gone camping in bad weather, the first shower you take when you get home is one of the sweetest ones you will ever know!

Try This

The next time you are about to get in your shower, perhaps reluctantly (if it is too early!), try this: just before you turn the knob/press the on-button for your shower, pause for a moment, and imagine if you lived in a poor part of the world with no indoor running water. Imagine having had to carry litres of water from a village well, perhaps miles away – and perhaps having taken several journeys to get enough to take a shower. Imagine the heat, the pain in your muscles from the weight of carrying the water. Just for a moment, put yourself in the shoes of the millions of people who need to do this. Take your breath, and now turn on your shower. As you stand underneath it, give gratitude for the place you live in, the home you have, where this water flows over your body at the touch of a switch. Consider this anchor thought: *Water is a gift.*

Appreciate the cleansing power of this water. As it washes over your face and head, know how very lucky you are.

You can also try this exercise when you turn on the tap in your kitchen to pour a glass of water. Be mindful of the ease of this, and that you have the choice to have instant clean water to drink. So many millions of people on earth literally die of thirst. Dehydration is a killer, and so is the absence of clean water. When we feel that not much in our life is going right, we can always remember to be grateful for the basics in life that we have to hand.

Fountains

Fountains might seem like a random addition to this section on bluespaces, but I wanted to talk about them because they represent ways in which humans introduce water into places that don't always naturally have them. The perfectly manicured landscapes of the historic homes of the European aristocracy almost always feature a fountain. Many of these have become tourist sites we go to see on holiday. There is a certain peace in taking a rest on a bench near a fountain when you are footsore from museum-fatigue. Many cities create fountains in their centres, in piazzas or near office blocks. They offer a focus for the eyes and the ears – the sight and sound of flowing water, cascading or sprinkling over interesting shapes and layers – that gives us rest for a moment. There have been many times on hot days on holiday when I have been sorely tempted to fling myself into a fountain – Paris in August, anyone?

Fountains often have historic importance as water sources for humans and horses – where they are seen as small 'fonts' in many European towns and villages. Many still function today, capturing local, fresh spring water. The funny joke in our family is that my partner's Italian surname translates directly as 'nasty fountain'. So, whatever his ancestors were up to in ancient times, we surmise it must have involved trying to poison people's water! But regardless of whether we are talking about old village fonts, the grand statue-adorned fountains of important towns and cities, or the blocky modern water flows of contemporary business districts globally, fountains are human features that we are drawn to. Making wishes for love by throwing coins into Rome's Trevi Fountain or eating a supermarket sandwich next to a small fountain in the park near your workplace at lunchtime – all add something extra to our experience of built environments. They represent an attempt to bring nature in, through water, which helps us to appreciate beauty, simplicity and calm.

EXERCISE
MINDFUL LISTENING TO FOUNTAINS

Next time you have an opportunity to look at or sit next to a fountain, try this mindful listening exercise. Our brains have a filtering part (that's a non-technical phrase) called our 'RAS' – reticular activating system – which is a network of neurons in our brain stem that interprets sensory information, or filters all the 'data' we receive every moment of our day. We can only cope with so much, so our RAS helps us to focus on or choose what we tune into.

When I am teaching this in my practical ChillSquad sessions, I bring in a kitchen sieve and we put rice and sugar (Rice And Sugar – RAS!) into it. Then I ask the children to listen to a recording of some music, or a spoken piece – and to notice but then tune out all the school noises around us, in the hallway or the playground. We shake the sieve until only the rice remains. The rice represents the sounds we want to focus on, while the sugar are those sounds we are letting go of, passing through our filter. This is an important mindful listening skill, because we do live in a world where there is often a lot of noise that we have no control over.

- When you are by your fountain, I want you to take a proper look at who else is around the fountain, if anyone, and what the surrounding environment is like. You can simply observe and label; for example: 'a group of tourists', 'some other workers', 'young people', 'tall office buildings', 'tourist shops' or 'some restaurants'. Breathe in and out as you name and notice the surrounding environment.
- Now, pay attention to all the sounds around you. Also name them: for instance, 'people chattering', 'traffic passing', 'child crying' – or whatever it might be in that moment, where you are. Breathe in and out; you are mindfully and non-judgementally observing and naming the sounds, not reacting to them.
- Next, focus on the sound of the water in the fountain. Really tune into it. If you like, you can touch the back of your neck, to symbolise activating your RAS! This acts as a physical anchor to work with your brain and breath, and to focus on what you want to tune in to, not the overload of sensory distractions around you.
- What can you hear when you tune in to the fountain? Is the water strong or gentle? Sprinkling? Gushing? Crashing? What does the water look like as it flows and as it lands on the water pooling below it? Spend a few moments breathing calmly, just focusing on the water sounds themselves.
- When you are ready to stop, reflect on how easy or difficult you found filtering out other sounds, when you intentionally directed your focus on only the fountain.

Mindful listening is a useful exercise to practise in your everyday life more generally too. It can help students cope with busy or noisy learning environments and aid anyone who works in an open-plan office, or who is trying to work at home with children or others in the house. I am someone who is always in search of a calm and peaceful environment – but my reality is often very different. Before I discovered mindfulness, I would find myself getting annoyed and overwhelmed by what I found to be intolerable noise everywhere I turned! This intentional auditory focusing and tuning out, engaging the RAS, has been really helpful and calming. Water too, by its very nature, is a peaceful and welcome sound, and one that supersedes other noise in our environment, in the loveliest possible way.

Designing Your Own Bluespace

If you are drawn to the sight and sound of water, you might want to think about creating your bluespace water feature in your home or garden. I won't attempt a full DIY discussion here, but you can use very simple materials to create something that is personal to you. YouTube can guide you through some simple steps. A small pond pump can be plugged in to a socket that will create a moving or trickling effect. You can fill a large ceramic or metal dish with water. These can be filled with natural or coloured stones. Small decorative features and water plants are to be found in most aquatic centres and pet shops that sell fish. It is really up to you and your own personal taste how you create your water feature.

If you are lucky enough to have a garden, you could try to make a small water feature outside to begin with, and if you enjoy it, you could make your bluespace larger, or create a pond. We moved to a new house recently, and the biggest hit with my children was the small garden pond, filled with fish, and a pump-generated waterfall. It is surrounded by wood and has rocks and water lilies of different shapes and sizes in it. It is a peaceful oasis of water to look at, sit beside and listen to.

Bluespace Musings

Whether our bluespace is wild and natural, or indoor and contained, it offers us something. An opportunity to feel our bodies, to pause our busy minds and connect with where we are. Sometimes this takes practice – this tuning in or switching off. Our wellbeing can be enhanced hugely if we learn to make habits of these connections. The principles we considered in Chapter 3 – of presence, non-judging, letting go, mindful seeing and listening, trust and patience – can all be applied to our different bluespace settings.

When we think of our love of the ocean or sea, we are invited to just be. When we think of the calm of a lake or pond, we can invoke stillness. Rushing rivers and waterfalls offer a moving-on and power that we can take something from if we need that sort of energy in this moment. Invigoration or relaxation in the waters of our home form rituals in our everyday lives that pep us up or wind us down. We can choose to be grateful for the curious wonder and gift of water when we remember how lucky we are. Water is not something to take for granted, nor is the beauty of bluespaces. The next chapter examines some of the ways we can make sure that they – and therefore, we – are looked after.

6

MINDING OUR BLUESPACES

Even though this is not a book about conservation, per se, looking after the bluespaces that make us feel well is a vital and important premise. I want to think about the way in which learning about bluespaces builds into our awareness of them and hopefully, therefore, our willingness to care for them. For many people, their way 'in' to an interest in the seas, oceans and beyond is through popular television documentaries or the programmes they watch as children. The media has brought the story of *Blue Planet* to a huge audience – much wider than the specialist botanists or naturalists of days gone by (see page 166). One little boy I taught in a school mindfulness programme some years ago said to me when he saw me in the hallway, 'Oh hurray, Catherine, are you here to do *minding-us*?' I giggled and told him that was the best interpretation of it I had heard so far. So in a way, I want to consider, finally, how we can think about wellbeing, mindfulness and bluespaces with this 'minding' hat on. A common Irish phrase when leaving someone's company is to call out 'mind yourself', instead of goodbye. I think it is a call to be aware and to take care. And this awareness – this caring, and *minding* – is so crucial if the bluespaces we love are to be looked after, not only for ourselves but for those who come after us.

Protecting our Bluespaces

There are many ways that nations and organisations can choose to protect their bluespaces. We have lots of 'designations', whereby boundaries are drawn on terrestrial or aquatic maps and declared protected areas. Some are global, suggested by UNESCO, others are EU driven, and many are arrived at within national policy guidelines of individual countries. The terminology alone is bewildering – the names of many begin with 'M', such as Marine Management Organisations (MMOs), Marine Conservation Zones (MCZs), Marine Protected Areas (MPAs) – and more, but you get the idea. Without going into a detailed policy analysis here, it is worth knowing that many protected areas are arbitrary and designed to act as an 'encouragement' of sorts to do the right thing. The UNESCO Biopshere programme and natural World Heritage Sites are just some examples. There are, of course, some legal directives that must be followed by governments and local authorities (about considerations such as protected species and water quality, for example), but many relate to issues that affect economic matters, such as fishing or harbour health and safety. Water tends to be a difficult element to police, protect and monitor, it seems. The idea that water can be owned is an interesting capitalist principle which a lot of people do not question – but one that causes many problems when it comes to who profits from it and whose responsibility it is to look after it. The two, sadly, don't always go together.

Whilst marine policy itself is broad and far ranging, its key concerns relate to fisheries and ports, coastal zone management, bathing water quality, the aesthetics of coastal landscapes, habitat and coastal leisure space conservation. Planning and policy narratives are now beginning to include wellbeing alongside the more traditional marine concerns, but there is scope for further integration. An embedded 'Bluespace Approach', which emphasises ways that whole coastal habitats/ecosystems/communities can deliver wellbeing is a strong policy foundation moving forward.

We need to think, therefore, not just of the water itself, but the entirety of bluespace. Bluespaces are layers of human and natural features, needs and hopes. We have seen already how wellbeing is multifaceted – comprising of physical, psychological, social and environmental elements. Therefore, our approach to looking after it must take into account how all of these factors interact with each other in our bluespaces. There is a lot of good research out there already on 'ecosystem services' (how the environment benefits humans) and 'valuing nature', but more is needed, especially with a bluespace-wellbeing focus.

Kelli's Story

While I was growing up in Devon, the sea was my playground, sanctuary and became my true soulmate. Travelling around the world scuba diving in my twenties, I realised my white Western privilege, so volunteered with Blue Ventures in Madagascar, doing marine conversation scuba diving research on the third largest barrier reef in the world. The beaches were littered in plastic, the corals were bleached and degraded due to global warming, deforestation and over-fishing. We did our best to help.

On returning to the UK, I founded Plastic Free Greater Brighton, using social media to promote behaviour change, help organise beach cleans and support local plastic free businesses. It didn't feel enough. Having learned about climate change at university in 1993, and watching successive governments not doing enough to halt catastrophic climate change, I was compelled to join Extinction Rebellion (XR) and take to the streets to disobey non-violently, civilly of course (with NVDA – non-violent direct action).

With my supportive and likeminded Salty Seabirds swim group, we created an 'XR logo' in the sea in December 2019 to highlight the rising sea levels that will completely flood huge parts of the UK, including the very spot where we swim. You have to protect what you love.

The Media and Bluespace

Sir David Attenborough, take a bow! *Blue Planet*, a documentary series commissioned by the BBC was the most watched television programme in the UK in 2017, and was also watched by 80 million people in China as well as millions of others worldwide. It created what was known as 'the Attenborough effect', and for a time, governments increased their environmental public profile. One research study showed that 88 per cent of people who watched *Blue Planet* changed their behaviour as a result. As one person put it, 'Once you've seen albatross parents feeding plastic to their chicks, there's no going back.' Giving up single-use plastic items in favour of reusable bags, cups and straws features highly as a positive change in our environmental consumer behaviour, but there is much still to be done. Television, film, social and printed media hold a lot of power in *how* bluespace protection is communicated – be that factual, unbiased, sensationalist or entertaining – and to whom.

Starting young is a key factor in moving bluespace conservation forward. The wildly popular children's television cartoon series *The Octonauts* (whose slogan is 'Explore! Rescue! Protect!') was initiated by two marine biologists who wanted to teach children about ocean creatures and conservation. The motley crew of animal characters carry out subsea missions in all kinds of marine environments, encountering many creatures, great and small, some with the most fantastic accents! But the message drips into tiny brains. Watching Captain Barnacles and his friends rescue a beluga whale from a melting polar ice cap teaches children the link between climate change and habitat loss. *Finding Nemo* and *Finding Dory*, the Hollywood blockbuster movies, have also brought the underwater world to millions of children across the planet. Encountering and playing with clownfish, blue tangs, stingrays, turtles and sharks in movies like these also give young people marine-literacy. An ability to name and recognise aquatic creatures is a great start towards creating bluespace awareness and care.

There has been a surge in reality-outdoor programmes too. As society changes, many need nature to be dramatic and exciting. Raging planets and savage earths abound! The thrill of risking your life in 'dangerous nature' is an audience winner, it seems. Programmes such as *Deadly 60* (which ranks species that can kill you, basically), *Survivorman, Running Wild with Bear Grylls, Marooned with Ed Stafford*, and many others of a similar genre are hugely popular worldwide. My own children love them, and there are worse heroes to have than those who know nature and how to survive in it. I wonder, though, about some of the underlying messages at times: this often seems to be about a very masculine approach to 'conquering nature' and dominating it somehow. This approach of course has long roots in the history of the idea of the 'frontier' and earlier colonial exploration, in which nature and unknown places are there to be found, subjugated and used by humans – often at the expense of others, and of nature itself. The old underwater 'discovery' genre of programmes – Jacques Costeau and, now, the Attenborough conservation-ethos of the *Blue Planet* episodes – sit alongside these adventure/survival shows. And make no mistake; ironically, our very survival is indeed now at stake, on this blue planet of ours.

Try This

Choose a programme or movie from those mentioned above and watch it with your family or friends. After it's finished, write down three things you learned from it or three key points. Then, together, decide on three things that you can do to help the environment; these can be things inside your home or outside of it. You might make a change, for example, to things you use, buy or recycle. You might go to your nearest bluespace and help to clean it up. Whatever you choose to do, translate your response to these programmes and films into actions in your own environment. Watching passively and feeling temporarily awful, but without taking any kind of action, is no longer enough if we are all to effect the real changes needed to save our planet.

People, Nature and Water

Our natural and human environments interact all the time. At a lakeshore, a riverside or on a beach, we can see the water itself, the plants, the wildlife and skies above us – but we can also see the buildings, the jetties, the piers, the groynes, the boardwalks, the road, the carparks, and ice-cream shops. We see variable mixes of all these things, the natural and human, depending on where we are. Remote places offer us more nature, while urban spaces will have lots of human features. These are where most of the world's populations are found, in these towns and cities. And many are built around bluespaces. Historic human settlements, chosen for their water, are now bustling, burgeoning and bursting at the seams.

So, if we are to continue to use and cherish water for our wellbeing, we need to think clearly about how we *collectively* interact with it. Those of us who use fresh and saltwater places regularly would seldom think to ruin our very own watery playgrounds. But for many, there is a dissociation between our own behaviours and the environment they are set within. Litter, pollution, plastic, waste management, water quality, climate change are all someone else's problem.

This neoliberal world is one where the individual is key, and where an interest in how community, government and policies work is at an all-time low.

However, not all reluctance to act or consume responsibly comes from a place of ignorance or indeed fecklessness. For many people, eco-anxiety is a real condition, especially the young. Eyes wide with fear, small children ask pertinent questions in the sessions I run, about whether we will all drown, or what happens when the clean water runs out... For some, the idea of trying to 'save the earth' or indeed 'save the oceans' is just too overwhelming. Too big. Too hard for one person to tackle. So, it is often easier to block it all out and carry on. All of these factors present huge challenges for how we are going to change the fate of our bluespaces and our planet.

All I can say with truth here is that our bluespaces need us – the waters themselves, the streams, the rivers, the rockpools, the seas, the lakes, the vast oceans and all the species, the big, small, the wow! creatures and the obscure ones. With our human impact, they can no longer self-regulate or self-sustain. We now need to protect them from *us*. Let that sink in.

The need to act is not a finger-wagging admonishment. To me, playing your part is just something that is decent behaviour. If we go to the sea, the lake or the river or swim in the oceans, then we must play a small part in looking after them or contributing somehow to their welfare. Imagine, if you will, someone who always goes to a party but never ever brings anything, doesn't help with the food or the preparation, offers nothing – but just cruises in, takes and enjoys all the goodies, in an entitled manner. Using bluespaces for our own benefit but contributing nothing, ever, is a bit like that, don't you think? Even if, up until now, we haven't really thought about it like that!

EXERCISE
THE NEED TO ACT

Anyone who has children at school, anyone who is environmentally aware, who is an activist or has studied science, geography or ecology, probably knows a reasonable amount already about what organisations are out there, helping our bluespaces. If you aren't familiar with any, then here is a little exercise to get you started...

In the same way that 'keep learning' is one of the Five Ways to Wellbeing, so too is it one of the ways of saving the bluespaces that are so central to our wellbeing. And that means you, me and all of us. Greta Thunberg's call to arms – to treat the climate crisis and our dying planet as if 'our house were on fire' – reminds me that the very thing we need to extinguish this fire is, in fact, *water*. So, what can we do?

- Adopt a tone and intention of curiosity and exploration here. (Scolding or scaring are not approaches that work for me when it comes to encouraging actions of change.)
- Ask yourself honestly, in this moment: Do I know what the big issues are about how bluespaces are being threatened a) globally, b) in my own country, c) in my own county/state and d) in my immediate local area? Rank yourself as 'knowing lots', 'knowing a little' or 'knowing almost nothing'.
- Reflect on your *love* of the water, and now think about your own ranking there. Does it feel OK? If it does, well done. If it doesn't sit that well, then ask yourself, what might *I* do about it? Right now? Short term? Long term?
- Make a list of organisations that might be relevant to bluespace protection. Then choose one global organisation (e.g. Greenpeace, UNESCO), one national (for your own country), and one local. Find out all you can about them. Think about 'passive' and 'active'

ways to get involved. Passive might be making a donation to a cause, or buying some merchandise from them that goes towards conservation work. Active ways might be to join a group, go to meetings, go to a talk, do a course, go on a climate change march, or work with others to take direct action. It is not my place to advocate one organisation or course of action over another here. This will depend on who you are, your interests and where you are.

- Make a written plan with your intentions and actions and *date each one*. Not all have to be external. You can take action within your own home or family too. Write those down too (examples: 'go to the Sussex Wildlife talk about the marine conservation plan next Thursday', 'take out membership of Greenpeace', 'join my local environmental-action group', 'buy my sister an Xtinction Rebellion T-shirt for her birthday', 'find and recycle all plastic waste in my kitchen this weekend', 'buy four litter pickers online and take the children to do a shoreline clean next Sunday').

Imagine if every household did this – if we all took responsibility for our actions, our consumption and made it our business to *understand* what is happening? If a loved one were sick, we would seek help, we would try find out what was wrong, and we would take action. Our blue planet is that loved one.

Ruth's Story

I've always been drawn to water, any water; rivers, lakes, tarns, streams and of course the sea. As a child, it was quite often too cold for me to actually swim but I spent a lot of my time splashing about, enjoying the sensation and happiness it gave me. From around the age of 25, I started surfing. Within any one session I would experience a myriad of emotions – from inner peace and tranquillity, to childlike excitement and pure stoke as the waves would pull me backwards then spit me out on what felt like, but probably didn't look like, a fast and turbulent ride. Invariably I'd let out a loud 'whoop', which in the surfing world isn't necessarily cool but I'd do it anyway, filled up to the brim with 'glad to be alive' feelings. I knew I was living my best life and that was all thanks to the sea.

As someone now nearing 50, the sea has become no less important to me and has taken on a more healing role as the stresses and strains of a fast-paced world take hold. I started sea swimming in May 2017 although I didn't see that winter through. My first winter was the year after and it was freezing! My body was burning in the cold water – it felt like someone was sticking pins into me, all over. Although it sounds painful, and it was, it was also addictive. However, my body started to adapt to the cold and it was fascinating to experience how it began to cope with the bitter conditions I started to regularly put it through. I felt giddy and alive in a way I never had before (not even when I surfed my first green wave). Having now completed my second winter sea swimming in just my swimsuit, hat and goggles, I feel my body and mind can deal with anything life throws at it.

The Covid pandemic lockdown of 2020 provided me with a time for reflection. The streets and, more importantly, the beaches were temporarily deserted. It felt like winter again, in a good way. Early each morning, I walked on the beach for my daily exercise and it was then that I began to notice the amount of plastic amongst the pebbles. I knew there had been an issue for years and I had been around people who had regularly collected three pieces of plastic before they left the beach ('take three for the sea'). I had never done this, instead had just grumbled at how inconsiderate people were leaving their rubbish. But the planet is our home and we must look after it. We must show it the respect it deserves and protect it passionately for the generations to come. So I decided to take my own action. I've just completed 100 consecutive days of beach cleaning by the sea where I live. I shall continue beyond my goal of 100 days now, as a thank-you to the sea for helping me to breathe each day and being the place where everything makes sense for me. In turn, I hope I too can help the sea to keep breathing.

How Wellbeing and Bluespace Conservation are Linked

Funnily enough, it was a paper I published on this very topic that led me here to this book, in a roundabout sort of way! I wrote an academic article in 2018 called 'I Need the Sea and the Sea Needs Me' for a marine policy journal.[1] I wanted to keep that title, soft and waffly as it probably sounded to an editorial board used to dealing with 'serious' marine matters. Why? Because I think it sums up perfectly this link between what the sea does for us, and how it too needs us to look after it in return. At my university workplace, as part of the Greenwich Maritime Centre, we had just run a conference called 'Society and the Sea', and my paper came from that. It was really interesting to see the spectrum of topics that the conference title threw up, ranging from fishing community heritage to shipwreck conservation.

For my part, I wanted to bring a wellbeing narrative to the table. It was a bit of a glaring gap, I thought, not to suggest that an obvious way to get people to take sustainable action on bluespaces that matter to them, was to just say 'look after the places that make you feel well'. The paper had a strong response and has since been picked up by various parts of the media, including the *Guardian* newspaper, a French filmmaker and various wellbeing/maritime organisations who have asked me to comment on these issues. It has been a great personal affirmation that if you follow your passion, and write about what you love, then good things often fall into place without forcing them. That work has put me in touch with lots of interesting people ever since and I feel very blessed because of it.

Interestingly enough, research is still relatively limited on the attempts to examine the symbiotic or reciprocal exchange of action, experience or behaviour of those benefiting from coastal wellbeing, and the potential for harnessing positive engagement with marine sustainability and education programmes. Things are changing for the better, though, as these ideas rise up the research-policy action agenda. Capitalising on this symbiotic relationship could increase the future sustainability of bluespaces. However, many people envisage huge sacrifices having to be made and there being some kind of trade-off between wellbeing and the environment, as if they were in conflict. Solid work on the concepts of 'marine citizenship', calling for the human care of the oceans, can be broadened to include wellbeing concerns too. These concepts of marine citizenship raise fundamental questions about the nature of social engagement with the sea. We can extend the idea of the marine to all waters too – a more general 'bluespace citizenship' perhaps?

I think education is key. In that paper, I called for the established of marine-education zones along all coastal seafronts – where people can consider and learn about what they are seeing or swimming in. We could apply this to rivers and lakes, to increase awareness. I know there are piecemeal attempts to do this – a billboard here, a picture there. But imagine if a whole region, or country, set up a coordinated approach to this education-communication of all bluespaces?

Many academics argue that a transition to sustainability requires a shift from materialist to post-materialist values, from anthropocentric to ecological worldviews. But perhaps the shift is not so stark? Perhaps humans are innately aware of the need to look after those bluespaces that they feel *connected* to, and that nourish them on physical, psychological and social levels? Public sector policy, I firmly believe, has a duty to protect bluespaces – as therapeutic landscapes and as conservation sites, simultaneously. What about some branded information signage, approved workshops, children's camps, action groups, liaison with existing organisations in a joined-up approach, and evening classes on bluespace joy and wellbeing? Well, we can dream, and put it out there...

EXERCISE
LEAVE NO TRACE

This is a basic clean-up of a shoreline you frequent: it might be the beach, a lakeside or a riverside, or even the pond in your local village. You can do this exercise as part of an organised group; there are many local action groups who often carry out clean-ups. A quick search online will throw up dates and locations. Just make the decision to join one! Or gather some friends, or your own family – and set a time and date to go to the shore and help to tidy it up.

- If possible, buy or borrow some litter pickers (kids love using these), and take five or six sturdy garbage bags with you. Decide which ones will be for general rubbish and which will be for recycling. Wear safety gloves to protect yourselves from glass, dog mess or other nasties.
- When you arrive at your shoreline, decide either on a spatial area to cover (groyne to groyne, cove to headland, rock to rock, tree to tree, for example), or a timeframe ('meet back here in one hour'). Work in pairs, preferably.
- As you pick up other people's litter, it is really hard not to feel anger, disappointment and sadness. But try to turn those emotions into a sense of pride – reframe them as helping the water and all the life that lives in it and depends upon it. Imagine this even if you can't see that immediate effect with your own eyes right now, as you are doing this great work.
- From time to time, don't forget to stop and breathe. Look out at the water and sky. Appreciate all the joy

---

it brings you. Think about the creatures that live in that water. Imagine them with smiling faces, surviving another day, because of *you*.

- When your time is up make sure that you know where to dispose of your collected garbage bags. Research this first, as it will differ from place to place.
- Give yourself and your team a pat on the back, and *know* inside yourself, that you have given something back. Don't be that party guest that just always takes. 'Give' is one of our Five Ways to Wellbeing, and it makes us feel good to help.

Note: Silent disco version! An excellent way to add that something extra to a beach-clean is to do it in a silent-disco format. There is nothing quite like grooving along to some excellent tunes with a set of headphones on while saving the environment! Watching others dance, sway and tap in time to a spot of litter-picking makes the whole thing huge fun. Check out your local options online.

In his *Blue Mind* book, Wallace J. Nichols veers away from quoting grim statistics about the polluted grey seas choked with plastic, and instead incites a positive attitude towards creating a love of the sea – and a nurturing of it that comes from within us all and our need for water as an essential part of our wellbeing. I too advocate this approach. If it matters to you, then be *active* about looking after your bluespace. 'You need the water. And the water needs you now. I wish you water', he says. It is a great sentiment. Now imagine the colour you want *your* water to be, imagine the purity of it, imagine the plants and creatures who need it to be clean, imagine the humans who need it be clean to drink it and to bathe or swim in it. You are that human. Take action, please.

CONCLUSION

FOR THE LOVE OF BLUESPACE

If I were to try to sum up what has been covered in this book, I'd say it is a call for a personal way of thinking about how our bluespaces help us. And for a way for that personal engagement to become collective, when needed. Wellbeing and water are intricately linked. Being in and near bluespace positively affects our bodies, our spirits and our minds. Throughout the highs and lows of life, water is a constant. I hope I've shared some of my own journey in water with you, and that you can identify with some of that and the shared stories of others who have beautifully contributed to the research and the conversations throughout.

We have talked about why bluespace matters, what it means to us, how it can help us to feel well, and what we can do to look after this aquatic-held space of ours. We can try the various exercises, practices and observations offered in each chapter when we are in or near water. Whether bluespace is our playground, our gym, our metaphorical therapy couch, or our sacred place, we can all gain something we need from water. Bluespace thinking is mostly about an outlook, an awareness of our own thoughts, actions and wellbeing when we are in these spaces. Intentionally noticing our breath, our connections or our emotions helps to give us richer experiences when we are in them.

Body rituals in bluespace can involve swimming, surfing, paddleboarding or just walking along a shoreline. Our abilities, our preferences and enjoyment of these will all differ depending on who we are and where we are. When our bodies feel well, we invite in the traits of strength, power and stamina. *Mind* rituals in bluespace help to clear our mental chatter. Pressing pause on our busy monkey minds allows our brains to rest and recharge. Water facilitates this through the very sight of it, the sound and feel of it – feeding our senses and bypassing the need to analyse it all. When our mind feels well, we invite in the traits of clarity, openness and positivity. *Spirit* rituals in bluespace may involve meditation, contemplation or other personal practices. Mindfulness, intentional breathing, or taking time to reflect, allow us to connect with our inner world, our authentic selves. When our spirit feels well, we invite in the traits of peace, perspective, purpose and calm.

EXERCISE
AN EVERYDAY BLUESPACE RITUAL

Even if you do not live near bluespace, you can connect with water in simple daily practices. We've looked at many different exercises and tips throughout this book, but here is a very simple tribute to water you can do anytime, anywhere.

- Upon waking, splash water on your face – and notice the transition from sleep to wakefulness. If you like, you can say, 'With this water I wake up', and 'With this water I feel fresh.' (Sending the message to your brain creates a neural pathway, and makes it so – even if you are still dazed and sleepy, try it!)
- Next – shower. As the water washes over you, notice the way that your body reacts, the feel of the water on your skin. Give gratitude for the flick of a switch or turn of a tap that sends you this water. If you like, you can say, 'With this water, today is new.'
- During the day, each time you pour yourself a glass of water, try to notice the water itself and the power it has to hydrate you. Connect with the earth that gave it to us. Imagine those who have no accessible clean water. As you drink your water engage with it, knowing that

it is keeping you alive. You can say simply, 'Water is life', when you have your drink.

- If you are able to see any bluespace in your daily travels to work, school or in your neighbourhood, just really pay attention to it, if only for a moment. Notice its colour, movement and sounds. Take a few calm breaths and simply appreciate it. If you like, you might silently want to just say, 'Thank you for being here.'

- At night, when you lie down to sleep, close your eyes, take three deep breaths, in and out, and silently repeat to yourself, slowly, 'Calm blue ocean, calm blue ocean, calm blue ocean...' See what thoughts, feelings and images come up for you. Allow your mind to quieten, and your body to fall asleep peacefully.

There are many rituals around bluespace that you can build into your own yearly calendar too. Holidays and days out to water appear in most people's lives – where you do what you fancy with the space and the weather you're given! But maybe you can begin other rituals too. Every Christmas Eve in our family, for example, we go together to our beloved little wooden beach hut on the Brighton seafront. We light a fire pit and bring fairy lights and flasks of mulled wine, and invite some friends to join us.

And ever since my children were very little, we've created 'Santa pebbles'. This is something I made up from my own imagination – and a canny manoeuvre to get my cold-hating Italian partner to brave the coastline in December! We go to the beach and look for flat, lighter coloured pebbles. And when we have one apiece, we take it and write our name on it, and decorate it – flowers, shapes, stars, it doesn't matter, whatever an eco-friendly marker-pen will allow. You can also buy eco-glitter, which will add sparkle to your pebble. I usually make a family pebble too – and then I arrange them all on a piece of drift wood, or surround them with seaweed, and have everyone sit for a photograph with them. Our collection looks like this: one pebble that says Daddy, one for Mummy, one for Luca, one for Jacob, and one that says 'Kelly family, Brighton, Christmas, 20xx' (the date being whatever the year is) – set out on the beach or on some other surface. If you don't celebrate Christmas, you can adapt this exercise to suit any meaningful festival or date that is important to you.

It is a lovely record of each year passing, and the children have got bigger with each passing pebble ritual. When we have taken our pictures, we then walk to the water's edge. The boys think of a wish for Santa Claus and we adults make a wish for ourselves, for the season, the holiday, or the year ahead, and on the count of three – One! Two! Three! – we all throw our pebbles far out to sea. Then Santa knows that the boys are ready, and he can come that night. The pebbles glint up at his sleigh and Rudolph's nose, and he winks down at us to let us know he is on his way. We have had a whole shoreline of friends and children do this, under the Christmas Eve night sky. Looking back on the photographs makes me well up every time, old softie that I am! Childhood innocence, togetherness, and the sea there, holding us all together in its own special way.

EXERCISE
SEASONAL RITUAL MAKING

Whatever your circumstances or beliefs, it's easy to create your own seasonal rituals.

- Get out your calendar and make note of the full moons, spring and summer solstices, family anniversaries or other dates that might be important to you. Make up your own ritual to suit the event you have in mind. You can decide it in advance, before you go to your bluespace – or you can be spontaneous and think of something when you get there. Suggestions might include:

- going for a full moon swim (if it safe to do so) at the exact time when the moon rises (you can easily check this online);
- remembering a lost loved one on their anniversary by making a nature-posy of grasses, weeds and twigs if you are by a lake, pond or river, or, if at the seaside, a pebble or shell with their name written on one side and the word 'love' on the other – and setting your posy, shell or stone out into the water, with a moment of reflection on the good things that person brought to your life;
- a shore-side fire pit (safely contained) to sit around and share stories, on the longest day of the year;
- a fountain wish: when you pass one, stop to make a wish for yourself, for a loved one and for the earth. Anchor the habit of doing this anytime you see a fountain. It makes you feel good!
- a New Year's Day swim or shore visit, to cleanse away the old year and invite in the new. If you like, you can write down three things you want to lessen, lose, or get rid of in the new year (such as 'fear', 'complacency', 'pain', or whatever is going on for you at the time). Imagine letting them go as you watch the water – or you can again physically write them down on a pebble or shell, and throw them into the sea, lake or river.

Ritual and traditions, especially the ones we make up ourselves, become part of our family stories, our personal stories, our identity. Bluespace facilitates so many stories, so many possible traditions.

My own story of water and bluespace was brought into sharp focus through a sudden tragic event. But it had begun before then too, in the lakes of Canada, the rivers and seas of eastern Ireland. And then the call to refuge and healing on the western Atlantic coast of Mayo. Solitude and bluespace there; then, balance regained, the next bluespace solace came from London's river Thames. And so, to Brighton – an everyday existence in bluespace that feeds my soul. There, with a community of other like-minded watery spirits and my own family, the sea is an ally and companion in our lives. Annual holidays and weekend escapes to swim and surf and plunge in my favourite bluespaces of Cornwall, Antrim, Mayo, Sagres, Famara, and many more places pepper my life with true blessing and deep connection to bluespace and those I share it with. I feel profound gratitude for having this love, this connection, to the water; because it brings me peace and balance wherever I go, always.

EXERCISE
MY WATER JOURNAL/JOURNEY

An interesting and cathartic exercise is write down a description of your own relationship with water – a journal activity if you like, or a water-journey account. You can write it free-flow, or keep it as a log-book to which you can come back and add more, maybe as part of your solo retreats. But I'd like you to start with recording your earliest memories of water in nature, and the changing relationship you may have had with it over time.

- Find a notebook, or you can buy a new one especially if you wish. Or create a new Word document in a digital file or folder and call it 'My Bluespace'. As well as writing and adding to your own journal, you can save useful links, articles, websites, groups, images, or anything about bluespace that piques your interest.

- You can write in any way you wish, but if some structure helps, try these headings:

  □ 'My First Memory of Water': think about where it was, who was there, and what you can remember about the experience.

  □ 'My Early Childhood and Water': see if you can remember the places you visited most with your family. What feelings can you remember?

  □ 'My Teenage Years in Bluespace': where did you go? What did you do? Did your relationship with the water change? How?

  □ 'Bluespace as an Adult': what is your relationship with water like now? How often do you go to bluespaces? What do you do there? How do they make you feel? *Why* do you go? With whom?

  □ 'Favourite Holiday Memories in Bluespace': where and why? Describe the water.

  □ 'My Most Frightening Experience with Water': what happened? How do you feel about that now?

  □ 'Bluespace First Aid': have you had any problems that bluespace has helped you with? For example, grief, depression, mental or physical health challenges, relationships? If so, how has it helped you?

  □ 'My Future Relationship with Water: what do you hope for?

This sort of journaling helps us to reflect on our own, very personal relationship with water. It will hopefully let you see how much bluespace matters to you.

A love of bluespace allows us to do so much. When we love the water, the nature around it, the landscapes and the creatures who share bluespace with us, we feel a unique sense of contentment. Water *lets* us do this — it lets us play, it lets us connect, it brings us calm. It is a unique element. I think it is a metaphor too, perhaps, for ourselves. At times we need to capture the strength, ferocity and power of water to get us through the hurdles that life throws at us. At times, we are knocked down and overwhelmed. Then, after surges of power, comes the need to be calm — a time of still water. In this stillness comes peace, recovery and rest. And so the cycle begins again, ebbing and flowing, rushing and quietening.

As our years pass, so too do our lives, and it is by paying attention to each moment, to each day that we learn to not live with regrets. Water in bluespace draws our attention inwards. It focuses us on what we are seeing, what we are feeling or hearing. Being with our breath, calming our minds, reframing our thoughts, soothing our bodies. Being in the present moment. Bluespace has so much to teach us, if we can quieten and listen…

ENDNOTES

Chapter 2

1. Department of Health, (2014). Wellbeing: Why it matters to health policy [online]. *GOV.UK.* [Viewed 14 September 2020]. Available from: https://www.gov.uk/government/uploads/system/uploads/attachment_data/file/277566/Narrative__January_2014_.pdf

2. Nuffield Health, (2017). Rate your wellbeing using this Wellbeing Wheel [online]. *Nuffield Health.* [Viewed 14 September 2020]. Available from: https://www.nuffieldhealth.com/article/rate-your-wellbeing-using-this-wellbeing-wheel#about

3. New Economics Foundation (NEF), (2011). Five ways to wellbeing [online]. *New Economics Foundation.* [Viewed 14 September 2020]. Available from: http://neweconomics.org/projects/five-ways-well-being

4. Kelly, C., (2017). Stress in the Higher Education sector: causes and yoga-mindfulness interventions. *Journal of Yoga & Physiotherapy.* **3**(3): 555613. DOI: 10.19080/JYP.2017.03.555613

5. Volker, S. and Kistemann, T., (2011). The impact of blue space on human health and wellbeing: salutogenic health effects of inland surface waters: a review. *Int. J. Hygiene and Environmental Health.* **214**, 449–460.

6. Walsh, J. and McGroarty, B., (2019). Prescribing Nature [online]. *Global Wellness Summit.* [Viewed 14 September 2020]. Available from: https://www.globalwellnesssummit.com/2019-global-wellness-trends/prescribing-nature/

7. BBC, (2020). The Wave begins surf-therapy pilot for anxious children [online]. *BBC News.* [Viewed 14 September 2020]. Available from: https://www.bbc.co.uk/news/uk-england-bristol-51836026

8. Foley, R., (2011). Performing health in place: the holy well as a therapeutic assemblage. *Journal of Health & Place*, **17**(2), 470–9.

9. Foley, R., Kistemann, T. and Wheeler, B. (eds.), (2019). *Blue Space, Health and Wellbeing: Hydrophilia Unbounded*. London: Routledge.

10. Gesler, W., (1992). Therapeutic landscapes: medical issues in the light of the New Cultural Geography. *Soc. Sci. Med.* **34**, 735–746.

11. Gesler, W., (1996). Lourdes: healing in a place of pilgrimage. *Journal of Health & Place*. **2**(2), 69–138.

12. White, M. P., Alcock, I., Wheeler, B. W. and Depledge, M. H., (2013). Coastal proximity, health and well-being: results from a longitudinal panel survey. *Journal of Health & Place*. **23**, 97–103.

13. Natural England, (2011). Monitor of Engagement with the Natural Environment. Annual Report from the 2010–11 Survey. Sheffield: Natural England.

14. Wheeler, B. W., White, M., Stahl-Timmins, W. and Depledge, M. H., (2012). Does living by the coast improve health and wellbeing? *Journal of Health & Place*. **18**(5), 1198–1201.

15. van Tulleken, C., Tipton, M., Massey, H. and Harper, C. M., (2018). Open water swimming as a treatment for major depressive disorder [online]. *British Medical Journal Case Reports*. [Viewed 14 September 2020]. Available from: https://doi.org/10.1136/bcr-2018-225007

16. Tipton, M. J., Collier, N., Massey, H., Corbett, J. and Harper, M., (2017). Cold water immersion: kill or cure? [online]. *Physiology*. [Viewed 14 September 2020]. Available from: https://physoc.onlinelibrary.wiley.com/doi/full/10.1113/EP086283

17. Beery, T. H. and Wolf-Watz, D., (2014). Nature to place: rethinking the environmental connectedness perspective. *Journal of Environmental Psychology*. **40**, 198–205.

18. Kearns, R. and Collins, D., (2012). Feeling for the coast: the place of emotion in resistance to residential development. *Journal of Social and Cultural Geography*. **13**(8), 937–955.

19. Game, A. and Metcalfe, G., (2011). My corner of the world: Bachelard and Bondi Beach. *Journal of Emotion, Space and Society.* **4**(1), 42–50.

20. Bell, S. L., Phoenix, C., Lovell, R. and Wheeler, B. W., (2015). Seeking everyday wellbeing: the coast as a therapeutic landscape. *Journal of Social Science & Medicine.* **142**, 56–67.

21. Ashbulby, K. J., Pahl, S., Webley, P., and White M. P., (2013). The beach as a setting for families' health promotion: a qualitative study with parents and children living in coastal regions in southwest England. *Journal of Health & Place.* **23**, 138–147. Available at: http://dx.doi.org/

22. Kelly, C., (2018). 'I need the sea and the sea needs me': symbiotic coastal policy narratives for human wellbeing and sustainability in the UK. *Marine Policy.* **97**, 223–231. Available at: https://doi.org/10.1016/j.marpol.2018.03.023

23. Harper, M., (2017). The Healing Madness of Sea Swimming [online]. *Head Talks.* YouTube. [Viewed 14 September 2020]. Available at: https://www.youtube.com/watch?v=0pXLF0sucDU

24. Van Tulleken, C., (2018). *The Doctor Who Gave up Drugs.* Available at: https://vimeo.com/314733567.

25. Hof, W., (2017). *Way of the Iceman: How the Wim Hof Method Creates Radiant, Longterm Health – Using the Science & Secrets of Breath Control, Cold-Training & Commitment.* Saint Paul: Dragon Door Publications.

26. White, M., Pahl, S., Wheeler, B., Fleming, L., and Depledge, M., (2016). The 'Blue Gym': what can blue space do for you and what can you do for blue space? *Journal of the Marine Biological Association of the United Kingdom,* **96**(1), 5–12. Available at: doi:10.1017/S0025315415002209

27. Nichols, W. J., (2018). *Blue Mind: How Water Makes You Happier, More Connected and Better at What You Do.* London: Abacus.

28. Kaplan, R. and Kaplan, S., (1989). *The Experience of Nature.* London: Blackwell.

29. Nichols, W. J., (2012). Exploring Our Blue Mind [online]. *TedX Talk, San Diego.* [Viewed 14 September 2020]. Available from: https://www.youtube.com/watch?v=7n95yIBq6jo.

30. Denton, H. and Aranda, K., (2019). The wellbeing benefits of sea swimming. Is it time to revisit the sea cure? [online]. *Qualitative Research in Sport, Exercise and Health.* Available at: DOI: 10.1080/2159676X.2019.1649714

31. Kelly, C., (2020). Beyond 'a trip to the seaside': exploring emotions and family tourism experiences. *Journal of Tourism Geographies.* DOI: 10.1080/14616688.2020.1795711

Chapter 3

1. Kabat-Zinn, J., (2013). *Full Catastrophe Living - Using the Wisdom of your Body and Mind to Face Stress, Pain, and Illness.* New York: Bantam Books.

2. Bleakley, S., (2016). *Mindfulness and Surfing: Reflections for Saltwater Souls.* Brighton: Ivy Press.

3. Fitzmaurice, R., (2018). *I Found My Tribe.* London: Vintage.

4. Seabirds, Brighton, blog available at: https://seabirdsdotblog. wordpress.com/

5. Kelly, C. and Smith, M., (2017). Journeys of the self: the need to retreat. In: Smith, M. and Puckzo, L. (eds.) *The Routledge Handbook of Health Tourism.* Abingdon: Routledge.

6. Fyfe, W., (2019). Women cold water swimming in the Gower to help menopause [online]. *BBC News.* [Viewed 14 September 2020]. Available from: https://www.bbc.co.uk/news/amp/uk-wales-47159652.

Chapter 4

1. Kelly, C. and Smith, M., (2017). Journeys of the self: the need to retreat. In: Smith, M. and Puckzo, L. (eds.) *The Routledge Handbook of Health Tourism.* Abingdon: Routledge.

2. For more information about 'Soul Saturdays by the Sea' and micro-retreats (my offering for members of the public to join me and participate in some water and wellbeing in real life), please see www.corejourneys.com for dates and locations.

Chapter 5

1. Gooley, T., (2017). *How to Read Water: Clues and Patterns from Puddles to the Sea*. London: Sceptre.
2. Drabble, M., Freud, E. et al, (2019). *At the Pond: Swimming at the Hampstead Ladies' Pond*. London: Daunt Books.

Chapter 6

1. Kelly, C., (2018). 'I need the sea and the sea needs me': symbiotic coastal policy narratives for human wellbeing and sustainability in the UK. *Marine Policy*. **97**, 223–31. Available at: https://doi.org/10.1016/j.marpol.2018.03.023

FURTHER READING

Deborah Cracknell, (2019). *By the Sea*. London: Aster Books.

Anna Deacon and Vicky Allan, (2019). *Taking the Plunge: The Healing Power of Wild Swimming for Mind, Body and Soul*. Edinburgh: Black and White Publishing.

Roger Deakin, (2000). *Waterlog*. London: Vintage Books.

Margaret Drabble, Emma Freud et al, (2019). *At the Pond: Swimming at the Hampstead Ladies' Pond*. London: Daunt Books.

Sylvia Earle, (2014). *Blue Hope*. California: National Geographic.

Ruth Fitzmaurice (2018). *I Found my Tribe*. London: Vintage Books.

Tristan Gooley, (2017). *How to Read Water: Clues & Patterns from Puddles to the Sea*. London: Sceptre.

Alexandra Heminsley, (2018). *Leap In: A Woman, Some Waves and the Will to Swim*. London: Windmill Books.

Jenny Landreth, (2017). *Swell: A Waterbiography*. London: Bloomsbury Sport.

Charlotte Milner, (2019). *The Sea Book*. London: DK Children. (For children.)

Joe Minihane, (2018). *Floating: A Return to Waterlog*. London: Duckworth Books.

Wallace J. Nichols, (2018). *Blue Mind: How Water Makes You Happier, More Connected and Better at What You Do*. London: Abacus.

Callum Roberts, (2013). *The Ocean of Life: The Fate of Man and the Sea*. London: Penguin Books.

Charlotte Runcie, (2019). *Salt on Your Tongue*. Edinburgh: Canongate Books.

Daniel Start, (2013). *Wild Swimming*. London: Wild Things Publishing.

Bonnie Tsui, (2020). *Why We Swim*. London: Rider Books.

Raynor Winn, (2019). *The Salt Path*. London: Penguin Books.

USEFUL RESOURCES

My organizations
I would be delighted to hear from you if you are interested in taking part in one of my workshops, talks or classes.

Blue Space retreats are one-day or weekend offerings focusing on a range of issues from general wellbeing, bereavement and stress management, to fun by the water. Soul Saturdays by the Sea is a new initiative of micro retreats allowing individuals and organizations to take a break for themselves in bluespace. Come and relax by the water; take time out for yourself to reset and relax.

Wild Blue School offers Blue Spaces learning for school groups and children. Knowing about how our coast works and what is in our seas makes us passionate about looking after them!

I also speak at organizational events, conferences and seminars in the health, education, environmental and private sectors across all aspects of wellbeing, stress, nature, sustainability and bluespaces.

For more information, please follow me on Instagram @bluespaces_uk or visit www.bluespaces.uk

ChillSquad
ChillSquad is a specific wellbeing programme I've developed to teach mindfulness and resilience to young people in education settings. I also work with families and train teachers and others who work with young people. Please visit en-gb.facebook.com/Corejourneys on Facebook.

Other helpful organisations

Aware

www.aware.ie

Support for depression and bipolar, courses, online advice and programmes for schools and workplaces. Ireland-based.

The Blue Gym Initiative

https://www.facebook.com/TheBlueGym

For updates and resources on how being outdoors in or near water helps our wellbeing.

Canadian Mental Health Association

cmha.ca

Support online and in Canadian towns and cities for a range of issues. Offers workplace and peer-support programmes.

Incredible Oceans

www.incredibleoceans.org

A non-profit organisation that promotes ocean advocacy, environmental learning, outreach programmes, education, festivals and much more.

Marine Conservation Society

www.mcsuk.org

A key ocean and seas conservation charity – lots of great information on beach cleans, campaigns, consumer information, education and courses.

Mental Health Australia
mhaustralia.org
A great gateway website for resources to access for a range of mental health and wellbeing areas.

Mind
www.mind.org.uk
A leading mental health charity in the UK. They offer advice and support for anyone experiencing mental health difficulties. They also campaign for mental health awareness in workplaces and society generally, destigmatizing depression and other mental health challenges. They run courses and workshops in many towns and cities.

National Institute of Mental Health
www.nimh.nih.gov
Leading US-based research organisation on mental health, offering lots of factual and evidence-based articles on various aspects of mental health and wellbeing.

Outdoor Swimmer Magazine
outdoorswimmer.com
This is a wonderful resource for anyone interested in bluespace swimming. There are tips on: places to swim; overcoming fears of deep water; events; swim gear; blogs and great, inspiring articles to read about people who love the water.

Outdoor Swimming Society

www.outdoorswimmingsociety.com

This is great for information on a whole range of things – places to swim, gear to wear, safety, events and more – and it is for both saltwater and freshwater swimming.

Royal National Lifeboat Institution (RNLI)

rnli.org

The key lifesaving organisation for the UK coastline. Visit for critical facts about how to stay safe in the water, information on how tides and rip currents work, distress signals and beach flags/lifeguard advice.

Surf Life Saving

sls.com.au and www.slsgb.org.uk

An organisation with many local coastal branches all over the world, including Australia and the UK, which trains people from as young as six years old to become beach lifeguards. It is an amazing group for children, teens and adults to join – offering fitness, surf skills, lifesaving, safety and conservation ethos all rolled into one, with a huge sense of camaraderie, community and group identity. (All the wellbeing elements in one, in other words – this organisation is a big part of my own family's life).

Very Well Mind

www.verywellmind.com

US-based organisation with lots of online resources, articles and advice for staying well mentally in all aspects of life.

ACKNOWLEDGEMENTS

I'd like to thank Jo Lal at Welbeck Balance for approaching me to write this book after spotting a timely article in the *Guardian* newspaper. She saw me for the odd hybrid that I am – an academic/researcher and a wellbeing practitioner! Her insight into how these two might merge gave birth to the idea for this book. I'd also like to thank Sue Lascelles, my editor, for all her wonderful help and encouragement. She has made this process a really positive experience for me, and she has kept me going through some pretty tricky writing circumstances.

I also want to thank Ale, for tolerating my writing-exits (mainly to the parked car outside the house!) and the stresses that come with plate-spinning work, writing and being a partner and a parent. To Luca and Jacob, my boys, my loves – thanks for putting up with mum and being quiet when she needed to write. Sharing my love of water with you both has been *one of the very best parts* of being your mother. Watching you play by the sea, learn to surf and go fearlessly and joyfully into bluespace makes my heart soar. Always go to the sea when you need peace and strength, my sweet boys.

I'd also like to thank my wider family for their support – to Ciara, Susan, Richard, my siblings, the legend that is 'Auntie Mary', and my cousin Kieran, who knew nature. My friends Jenny, Jude, Alex, Emma, Daisy, Charlotte and Lucy in Brighton, Nikki in London, Julie and Caitriona in Ireland, Dawn in Switzerland, and Kerry in the US – who listened, encouraged and kept me going.

For me, one of the loveliest and most life-affirming encounters I've had has been joining Brighton's Salty Seabirds swimming group. This 'salted wellbeing' gathering of like-minded souls who brave the cold and choppy waters of Sussex in joy, support and solidarity, all year round. You've listened, laughed and shared your stories, your warmth, tears, hugs, raucousness and cake. You know who you are. You are all mad, and I love you dearly!

We are the sum of our parts, and everyone mentioned here matters to me and has helped with this book in one way or another. Thank you all.

TriggerHub.org is one of the most elite and scientifically proven forms of mental health intervention

Trigger Publishing is the leading independent mental health and wellbeing publisher in the UK and US. Clinical and scientific research conducted by assistant professor Dr Kristin Kosyluk and her highly acclaimed team in the Department of Mental Health Law & Policy at the University of South Florida (USF), as well as complementary research by her peers across the US, has independently verified the power of lived experience as a core component in achieving mental health prosperity. Specifically, the lived experiences contained within our bibliotherapeutic books are intrinsic elements in reducing stigma, making those with poor mental health feel less alone, providing the privacy they need to heal, ensuring they know the essential steps to kick-start their own journeys to recovery, and providing hope and inspiration when they need it most.

Delivered through TriggerHub, our unique online portal and accompanying smartphone app, we make our library of bibliotherapeutic titles and other vital resources accessible to individuals and organizations anywhere, at any time and with complete privacy, a crucial element of recovery. As such, TriggerHub is the primary recommendation across the UK and US for the delivery of lived experiences.

At Trigger Publishing and TriggerHub, we proudly lead the way in making the unseen become seen. We are dedicated to humanizing mental health, breaking stigma and challenging outdated societal values to create real action and impact. Find out more about our world-leading work with lived experience and bibliotherapy via triggerhub. org, or by joining us on:

🐦 @triggerhub_

f @triggerhub.org

📷 @triggerhub_